CARRIAGES
AND
SLEIGHS

200 ILLUSTRATIONS FROM THE 1862 LAWRENCE, BRADLEY AND PARDEE CATALOG

LAWRENCE, BRADLEY & PARDEE,

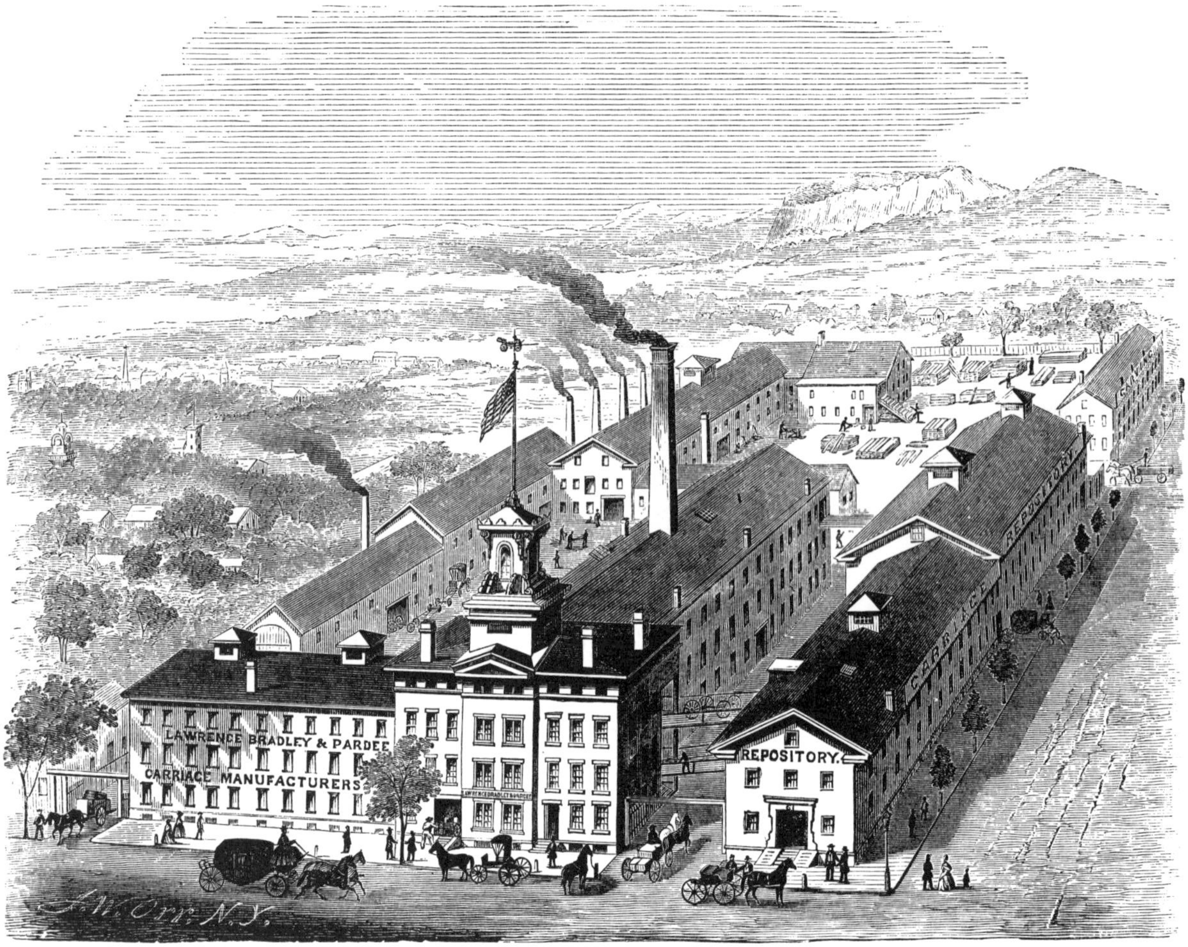

JOHN R. LAWRENCE. WM. H. BRADLEY. WM. B. PARDEE.

Carriage Factory and Repository,

Nos. 61 to 67 CHAPEL STREET,

NEW HAVEN, CONN.

U. S. A.

CARRIAGES
AND
SLEIGHS

200 ILLUSTRATIONS FROM THE 1862 LAWRENCE, BRADLEY AND PARDEE CATALOG

Lawrence, Bradley and Pardee

Introduction by Don H. Berkebile

DOVER PUBLICATIONS, INC.
Mineola, New York

Published in Canada by General Publishing Company, Ltd., 30 Lesmill Road, Don Mills, Toronto, Ontario.
Published in the United Kingdom by Constable and Company, Ltd., 3 The Lanchesters, 162–164 Fulham Palace Road, London W6 9ER.

Bibliographical Note

This Dover edition, first published in 1998, is an unabridged republication of the work originally published by Lawrence, Bradley & Pardee of New Haven, Connecticut in 1862 as their illustrated catalogue. A new introduction has been written especially for this Dover edition.

DOVER *Pictorial Archive* SERIES

Library of Congress Cataloging-in-Publication Data

Lawrence, Bradley & Pardee (Firm)
Carriages and sleighs : 200 illustrations from the 1862 Lawrence, Bradley & Pardee catalog / Lawrence, Bradley & Pardee.
p. cm.
Reprint. Originally published under title: Illustrated catalogue of carriages, sleighs, harness, saddles, etc. New Haven, Conn. : Lawrence, Bradley & Pardee, 1862.
Includes index.
ISBN 0-486-40219-3 (pbk.)
1. Lawrence, Bradley & Pardee (Firm)—Catalogs. 2. Carriages and carts—Connecticut—New Haven—Catalogs. 3. Sleighs—Connecticut—New Haven—Catalogs. I. Title. II. Title: Illustrated catalogue of carriages, sleighs, harness, saddles, etc.
TS2033.L39 1998
688.6—dc21 98-7047
CIP

Manufactured in the United States of America
Dover Publications, Inc., 31 East 2nd Street, Mineola, N.Y. 11501

ILLUSTRATED CATALOGUE

OF

CARRIAGES,

SLEIGHS,

HARNESS, SADDLES, &c.

COMPRISING OVER TWO HUNDRED OF THE FINEST AND MOST CORRECT CARRIAGE ENGRAVINGS EVER PRODUCED;

TO WHICH IS PREFIXED

A FULL DESCRIPTIVE LIST.

BY

LAWRENCE, BRADLEY & PARDEE,
NEW HAVEN, CONN., U. S. A.

1862.

PRINTED BY
JOHN W. ORR,
Engraver on Wood and Printer,
No. 75 Nassau Street,
NEW YORK.

ELECTROTYPED BY
LOVEJOY & SON,
15 Vandewater street,
NEW YORK.

INTRODUCTION

The broad selection of fine carriages shown in this 1862 catalog of Lawrence, Bradley & Pardee not only represents the line of one of New Haven's best-known carriage manufacturers, but shows as well practically all of the types of carriages that were popular in America at the time. Successors of the famed James Brewster, who initially gave the city its reputation as a carriage-building center, the three partners were not long to continue their association. In 1868, the original Brewster partner—John R. Lawrence—sold his interest to Bradley and Pardee, and in 1871 Pardee sold out to Bradley. After a few years, Bradley was forced to suspend operations. But a short time later, in about 1873, he sold the property to A. T. Demarest, who again succeeded in turning the factory into one of the city's leading establishments, at times employing as many as 200 men. In 1915, A. T. Demarest & Co., now engaged in both carriage and automobile work, ceased to exist.

This catalog was originally published at a time when the initial effects of the American industrial revolution were first being felt by the carriage industry. While some rather basic machinery had come into use in the industry as early as the 1830s and 1840s, and infrequent instances of parts manufacture could be found even earlier, the construction of a carriage still involved a great deal of highly skilled hand labor. This is borne out by a writer in *The Hub*, who wrote in 1897, "Twenty-five years ago one of the questions that was agitating the trade was, can machinery, other than for sawing, be used to an advantage in the carriage shop? [A]nd the consensus of opinion was that it could not, except where the capacity of the factory was such as to require four fires at least in the blacksmith shop."

Prior to 1862, wheel-making machinery had come into use, which certainly shaved the price of wheels, and consequently of carriages. Yet the gradual decrease in price that resulted from improved methods of mass production had only begun by 1862. A rather ordinary buggy cost nearly seven months of a tradesman's wages in 1862, exclusive of horse and harness; yet a comparable vehicle cost just over a month's wages by 1900.

This meant that the carriage, even one as unsophisticated as a buggy, was far from a household item in the 1860s, for the average working man had not the means, nor even much need for his own carriage. At the same time, the farmer had infrequently felt the need to own a pleasure vehicle, for he could use his farm wagon in lieu of a carriage. But it was not until the introduction of cheap buggies in the "three for a hundred" price range that many farmers thought of indulging in such a luxury. Thus, while scores of carriages might be seen in photographic and lithographic views of the 1860s, many a block in urban residential areas did not number a single carriage; and the workaday farm wagon was the only vehicle to be found on countless farms.

❦

The colors and fabrics used with these carriages of the 1860s are of special interest to modelers, restorers, and artists, yet the early catalogs seldom mentioned these. During this period, black—which became the leading color by the end of the century—was certainly in the lead for most classes of vehicles. Yet black carriages were probably outnumbered collectively by a variety of brighter colors.

Bismarck brown, and other dark to medium browns, were the most popular colors of this time for many classes of vehicles, excluding sporting vehicles. They appear to have been most favored after black. Both body and running gear might be of one color; or often, the two units might be different colors. A black or dark blue body might appear on a brown gear, or perhaps a brown body on a black gear.

Another popular color series consisted of various reds including lake, carmine, and vermilion, these again being applied to either body or gear. In the heavier classes, the lakes were most popular for bodies, often approaching purple; while in the lighter classes of vehicles, the carmines were used on both bodies and gears. Lake bodies on black gears were popular for the heavier vehicles. Buggies frequently had black bodies on carmine gears, yet all parts might be either carmine or black. Panels were frequently a different color from moldings, and an occasional special panel was likely to be some bright color. The belt-rail too was likely to be at variance, often black like the moldings.

Dark and medium blues also saw use; and in some instances, the darker greens, though these were not as common as they were in later years. Due to an awareness of the presence of arsenic in some shades of green, the use of that color was delayed for a time. Creams and yellows were occasionally used almost always on gears, and particularly on sporting vehicles such as dog carts. The reds were also popular colors for sporting vehicles; yet even here, black was evident. Among all classes of vehicles, numerous body-gear color combinations could be found.

The most striking feature of carriage painting at this time was the colorful striping, considerably more prominent than at a later time. Bodies were sometimes not striped, or again, might have modest striping—often in gold—on the moldings. The gears, however, were heavily striped, sometimes in only one color, but most often in two colors, or even three. A heavy stripe was often laid down first, over which finer stripes of another color or colors were laid. The latter centered or edged the broad stripe, or were sometimes set in slightly from the edges. Black and shades of red were frequently used, along with white, blue, and gold. Brown, yellow, purple, orange, and green were also to be seen. Buggies were often picked out with carmine and gold.

The most common trimming material was dark blue or blue-black broadcloth. Brown was less common, and dark green was infrequently used, for it had not yet gained the popularity it would later enjoy. Some of the heavier, more elegant carriages boasted satin or morocco trimmings, often in maroon. Sporting carriages were generally trimmed with drab corduroy or some other dull cloth, or sometimes with leather. A sleigh was often attractively trimmed with figured Brussels carpet. The carriage builder was careful, in any instance, to harmonize his colors with regard to body and gear colors, striping, and trimming.

For the benefit of model builders and artists, it should be noted that while these illustrations are comparatively accurate scale drawings, many carriage draftsman apparently felt that the drawing became too complex if the proper number of spokes were shown. Consequently, they simplified their work by decreasing the number.

Carriage wheels usually had fourteen spokes in each front wheel, and sixteen in the rear as some of the illustrations show. However, if the wheels were small enough, two spokes less per wheel would be appropriate. If the wheels were nearly the same size, they might have the same number of spokes.

Wheel track varied from fifty-four to sixty inches, and occasionally beyond these limitations according to prevailing custom in the area where the carriage was to be used. This allowed a body from forty to fifty inches wide on the heavier work, or down to thirty inches or less on the lighter work.

Today, the growing interest in horse-drawn vehicles—together with the general scarcity of accurate illustrations—clearly indicates the need for reproducing this splendid selection of Lawrence, Bradley & Pardee. It represents the extensive variety of carriages that were available in 1862 to those fortunate enough to be able to purchase one.

Don H. Berkebile

PREFACE.

In introducing this book to the Public, we desire to say a few words in regard to ourselves and our manner of doing business. Having existed over half a century, we trust it will not be deemed egotistical should some little pride for the past be shown, while high hopes are anticipated for the future.

Our business was established in the year 1810, by Mr. James Brewster, at New Haven, Ct. and carried on by him alone for nearly twenty years. During this time large consignments of Carriages were sent to Boston, Charleston and New Orleans; while a trade was commenced with Cuba, Mexico, and South America, which soon became a prominent part of the business. In the year 1827 he opened a Repository in New York City, and employed Mr. John R. Lawrence as Salesman until the year 1829, when a partnership was formed under the name of "Brewster & Lawrence." In 1830 Mr. Solomon Collis, who had been Mr. Brewster's bookkeeper since the year 1821, was made a partner also, and, until the year 1839, the firm was "Brewster & Collis" at New Haven, and "Brewster & Lawrence" in New York. It was under these names that the great reputation for the beauty and quality of the work was first attained, and which, we believe, has been constantly increasing.

On the first of February, 1837, Mr. Brewster retired from the firm. He is still enjoying in private life, at the ripe old age of seventy-four, a rich competency, the reward of honesty, energy, and industry. The business was then conducted under the name of "Lawrence & Collis" in New York, and "Collis & Lawrence" in New Haven, until the year 1850, when, owing to ill health, Mr. Collis sold his interest in New Haven to Mr. William H. Bradley, and in New York to Mr. Lawrence. The latter, soon after, connected with himself Mr. S. A. Durbrow, and his son, Mr. John Lawrence, under the firm of "John R. Lawrence & Co.," while at New Haven the firm was "Lawrence & Bradley" until January 1857, when Mr. William B. Pardee became a partner, under the name of "Lawrence, Bradley & Pardee." The Factory then was enlarged to its present size and beautiful proportions—a perfect model for convenience—more than doubling its former manufacturing facilities : facilities which are not surpassed, if equalled, by any other Carriage factory in the country.

During these fifty-two years every variety and style of vehicle have been built, from a child's Carriage up to the largest and most expensive Coach, and sent to nearly every part of the civilized globe. As our trade has become so extended, we find by experience that very few persons care to spend their time and money for travelling any great distance to select and purchase a Carriage. For this reason we were induced to go to the great expense we have incurred for the

best engraved, most correct, and largest collection of "Carriage Cuts," ever presented to the world; and for the attainment of which we are greatly indebted to the engraver Mr. J. W. ORR. We think all, who have had any experience in procuring Carriage engravings, will readily acknowledge their superiority to anything heretofore published. And although we present more than *Two Hundred Cuts*, yet these comprise but a part of the styles we are constantly manufacturing. There is scarcely any kind of a Carriage that we are not, at all times, prepared to build.

With only a Cut of a Carriage it is impossible to give more than a faint outline of its real finish—many an inferior one looking just as well on paper as the most expensive. Yet we trust every one can form some correct ideas from the engravings and descriptions, sufficient to determine at least upon the style and general finish desired. Decide this point first, and then, what is fully as important, send us your order, in which please give a full description of your wants. State the width of track required; height of wheels and body; whether to be light or heavy; with or without perch; plain or showy; color of painting, trimming, stitching, and plating; whether with shafts, or pole only, or both; the kind of axles and springs; whether designed for rough, hilly, sandy, or smooth roads; the material for trimming—leather, cloth, silk, etc.; if with top whether close or open. In fact, there is no danger of being too minute in giving your order. All we ask is to KNOW your wants, and then we have no fears as to a satisfactory result.

As for the *quality* of our work, we feel that little need be said, since we have the amplest testimony from every quarter, that, for variety of style, beauty of finish, and durability, our work has never been excelled. Our aim has always been to employ the very best workmen by the hour, instead of piecing the work out, as is customary in almost every other Carriage Factory. Consequently there is no excuse for the workmen slighting anything, or not doing their work in the best possible manner. If any are incompetent, they soon know that "their room is better than their company."

Each department is under a foreman of superior qualifications and experience, with strict instructions that nothing is to be used but the best, and nothing made in an imperfect manner. The Heavy and Light Work are manufactured under two distinct heads, in separate parts of the Factory, and by experienced workmen in each particular branch. Thus nothing is made without receiving that special attention required to make a perfect article of its kind.

We wish particularly to call attention to the fact, that owing to the very great and increasing demand for our Light Work, we have of late enlarged our facilities for manufacturing the same, and are now able to furnish, at short notice, not only every variety herein presented, but later styles, which we are constantly producing. It is our determination to remain, where we always have been, at the head of our profession.

REPOSITORIES.

Another most important feature in our business, to which we would call especial attention, is the

STOCK OF FINISHED CARRIAGES

always on hand in our New Haven and New York Repositories. At John R. Lawrence & Co., No. 410 Broadway, New York, can be found one of the largest and best selected assortments in that city; while at New Haven we have a Repository, three stories, 45 by 200 feet, the first floor filled with Heavy, and the others, with Light Carriages. We only reiterate the constant remark of all visitors, when we assert that, *for variety of styles, beauty of design, excellence of finish and quality, and amount of value represented*, our stock of Carriages excels any other collection in the world. From this no one can fail to see the great advantage purchasers possess in selecting from so large a collection, since they would be almost certain to find the very article sought for, already finished.

In conclusion, we submit our book to the Public, trusting that it will prove of mutual benefit both to the Purchaser and Manufacturer.

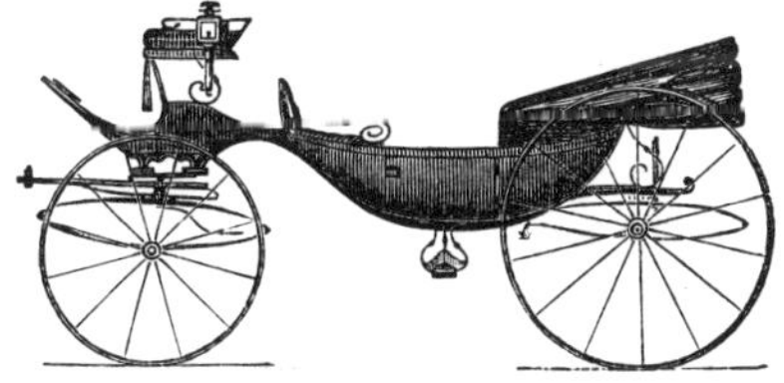

ALPHABETICAL INDEX.

DESCRIPTIVE LIST.

Note.—*We have commenced our List with No.* 101, *so as not to conflict with former publications.*

No. 101.—*Extra Fine Close Coach.* Full size; hung on loops, and C springs; with Salisbury boot and hammer-cloth; concealed steps; footman standard; spring backs and cushions; spring curtains; trimmed with the finest silk goods.

102.—*Medium Size Close Coach.* With French boot; trimmed with either fine cloth or silk; a most sensible Carriage throughout. The same kind of Coach can be made with shifting front quarters of either glass or wood.

103.—*Fine Full Size Coach.* French boot; hung on C springs; footman standard, and concealed steps. Finished plain but very rich.

104.—*A very Rich Glass-Quartered Coach.* Hung on loops; with Salisbury boot and hammer-cloth; steps which open and close with the door; iron baggage rack; trimmed in the very best manner throughout, and full plated.

105.—*Full Swept Coach.* Medium size, with shifting glass front quarters; drop light in back quarters; French boot; footman stand and holders; scroll irons; spring backs and cushions; finished in the best manner in every respect. It is a Coach that looks well, either showy or plain, and is never out of style.

106.—*Close Coach.* Same as No. 105, with the exception of panel in back quarters.

107.—*A Full Size Open Top Coach.* With French boot; large footman stand, suitable for baggage rack; an extra cover to go over the top when closed; ornamented. plated, and trimmed in the most gorgeous manner; but, of course, can be made as modest as any one may desire.

108.—*Sociable Caleche Coach.* Shifting front quarters; full plated; ironed and trimmed very elegantly. A very roomy, yet one of the lightest and most elegant Coaches that can be made.

109.—*Scroll Back Quarter Caleche Coach.* With half boot; shifting front quarters; well plated and thoroughly finished in every particular.

110.—*Light American Caleche.* Compass front; full boot; plaited movable ray-board; splash fenders over back wheels; hung on C and elliptic springs; spring backs and cushions; usually trimmed plain but elegant, and beautifully finished throughout. This is one of the easiest, and most comfortable Carriages, that can possibly be made; and when the top and frames are removed, it is, with the half-top, a most elegant open Carriage.

111.—*Full Size Round Bottom Caleche.* French boot; splash fenders; spring backs and cushions; very handsome lamps; made of the very best material throughout; finished plain but rich.

112.—*Light American Caleche.* Similar to No. 110 in every respect, except that it is not hung on C springs.

113.—*Scroll Back Quarter Caleche.* With half boot; made very showy throughout; of the best material and well plated. A most desirable summer Carriage with the half-top.

114.—*French Light Curtain Coach.* With full boot; O G front quarters; spring backs and cushions; made plain but nice.

115.—*Curtain Coach.* O G back and front; attached boot. A very light and most desirable Coach for six persons.

116.—*Crane Neck Caleche.* Very light; made either plain or showy. A very desirable Carriage for winter or summer use.

117.—*Light Crane Neck Caleche Coach.* Medium size; full plated, showy, and nicely trimmed throughout.

118.—*Caleche Coach.* With half boot; on four springs, with perch; roomy, and showy, inside and out.

119.—*Light High Door Coach.* Scroll back quarters; on four springs, with perch; can be finished either plain or fancy.

120.—*Very Light Caleche Coach.* Scroll back quarters and compass front; made showy; hung on four springs, with perch.

121.—*Child's Gig.* Hung on C and elliptic springs; leather top; trimmed with the best of silk. It is so arranged, that the child can ride with the greatest comfort either in a sitting or lying posture. In fact, for beauty, ease, and comfort, it is the *ne plus ultra* of anything in the Carriage line for children.

122.—*Child's Phaeton.* On C springs; prunella top; trimmed with silk. An exceedingly handsome and comfortable little Carriage.

123.—C *Spring Coach.* With hammer-cloth; can be made either showy or plain. A most desirable Carriage for a rough uneven country.

124.—*Child's Chaise.* With double joints, and side curtains to roll up. Universally used.

125.—*Crane Neck Caleche Coach.* On four springs, with perch; trimmed with either cloth or silk; made showy or plain.

126.—*High Door Coach.* Scroll back quarters; half boot; fancy ironed, and elaborately carved; trimmed with either silk or cloth.

127.—*Child's Chaise.* Single joints; roll-up curtains. An article that affords a great amount of happiness for a very little money.

128.—*Chariot.* Hung on C springs and loops; Salisbury boot, with splendid hammer-cloth; handsome carved footman standard; concealed steps; splash fenders on doors; trimmed in the best possible manner with silk goods; contains a concealed front seat, suitable for children; in fine, one of the richest appearing and most comfortable Carriages seen in the street.

129.—*Clarence.* Full size; on C springs; full boot; concealed steps; splash fenders on doors; finished similar to No. 128. There is nothing superior, in the Clarence line, in market.

130.—*French Clarence.* With round bottom; French boot; swelled back; carved back bar; fender straps; splash fenders on doors; finished throughout in the best manner.

131.—*Coupe.* Large size; full boot; swelled back; splash fenders on doors; concealed front seat for children; carved back bar; spring back and cushion; trimmed with the best of goods.

132.—*Coupe.* Medium size; for one or two horses; compass form; full boot; concealed front seat for children; carved back bar; fender straps; spring back and cushion; trimmed in the best style.

133.—*Light French Coupe.* Generally used with one horse, but arranged for one or two horses; full boot; hung very low, without steps; finished in the best manner throughout. This is a most desirable Carriage for ladies shopping or calling, or for a physician's use.

☞ Either size of the *Coupes* we can furnish with the French, half, or full boot, as we have a variety of bodies always finished, and painted various colors.

134.—*French Caleche.* Compass front; half top; hung on loops and C springs; Salisbury boot; concealed steps; front lid hung with concealed hinges; splash fenders on body and top; storm boot to protect the front seat. This is a very roomy, yet light, and exceedingly stylish Carriage, trimmed and finished in the most elegant manner—the *ne plus ultra* of a half-top Caleche.

135.—*Loop Barouche.* Round bottom; full top; full plated; egg boot; iron baggage rack; spring backs and cushions; finished in the best manner throughout. A most desirable Carriage for either private or livery use.

136.—*Sociable Half-Top Caleche.* Hung on C springs; full boot; concealed hinges to front lid; splash fenders on body and top; finished plain but in the richest manner. This is an entirely new style of Carriage. The door extends to the bottom of the body, presenting a much lighter full-swept carriage than can be obtained in the old way.

137.—*Sociable Half-Top Caleche.* Similar in every respect to No. 134, with the exception of C springs.

138.—*Barouche.* With O G front quarters; half boot; Caleche glass doors; full top; splash fenders over back wheels; iron baggage rack; scroll irons full plated; light, roomy, and stylish. A good winter, as well as summer, Carriage.

139.—*Gladstone.* Full boot; half top; storm boot to protect the front seat; splash fenders on body, front, and back; spring back and cushions; finished in the best manner throughout. This is a late style of Carriage; light but roomy; extremely liked by those who have used it.

140.—*Crane Neck Brett.* Full size, yet a very light and graceful article; concealed hinges to front lid; carved footman stand; scroll irons plated; spring back and cushions; storm boot; trimmed as may be desired.

141.—*Caleche.* Full swept; half top; French boot; footman stand; splash fenders on body; front lid with concealed hinges; spring backs and cushions; storm boot; elegantly finished throughout.

142.—*Light Crane Neck Barouche.* Full top; footman stand; irons scrolled and plated; spring cushions and back. A most desirable Carriage for summer or winter.

143.—*Caleche.* Full swept; full boot; half top;

splash fenders on body and top; concealed hinges on front lid; storm boot; spring back and cushions; finished in the very best manner in every respect. This style of Carriage is always fashionable, where half top Caleches are used.

144.—*Crane Neck Brett.* Medium size; gipsy top; footman stand; spring back and cushions. This is a very light and graceful Carriage; one that we can put on very high front wheels if required. We make a size larger of this same pattern.

145.—*Light Britzska.* Full boot; concealed hinges to seat lid; storm boot; spring back and cushions. This is an exceedingly stylish Carriage, finished elegantly throughout, and can be made plain or showy.

146.—*Light Half-Top Barouche.* Scroll back quarters; footman stand; storm boot; spring back and cushions. Those who wish to do their own driving will find this a very suitable Carriage, as the driver's seat is but a trifle higher than the back seat.

147.—*Crane Neck Brett.* Very light; roll up top; footman stand; spring back and cushions. Can be made plain or very showy, and is a beautiful Carriage finished in either manner.

148.—*Shifting Seat Brett.* For one or two horses; middle seat for children with a lid; spring back and cushion to back seat. No. 149 represents this Carriage with seats reversed, changing the whole appearance and style of the original, and making a very convenient and most desirable Carriage. A *multum in parvo.*

149.—*Shifting Seat Brett.* Showing No. 148 with seats reversed.

150.—*Cabriolet.* For one or two horses; on perch; spring cushions and back; middle seat on hinges, for one or two children; storm boot; splash fenders over back wheels; finished in the best manner in every particular. The cut represents a Carriage weighing about 500 lbs., but this article can be made much heavier, and with roll up top, footman stand, etc. For beauty and convenience there is nothing of its kind surpassing it.

151.—*Dickey Seat Brett.* For one or two horses; with perch; middle seat on hinges and drops, affording room for two medium-sized persons; storm boot; footman stand; wheels run under to perch. This is a light and most desirable Carriage, one that is extensively used in the West Indies, South America, Australia, as well as in the States.

152.—*Gipsy Brett.* This article is very similar to No. 151, except about the front seat; in other respects, not quite as expensive

153.—*Cabriolet.* For one or two horses; on perch; roll up top; finished in the very best manner, and weighing only 475 lbs. It, of course, can be made much heavier if required. This is a handsome Carriage as represented, or with extension top as No. 209. The style is new and elegant.

154.—*Loop Victoria.* For one or two horses; on perch; roll up top; splash fenders; large storm apron; showy lamps; wheels run under to perch. This is a very roomy and comfortable article, made strong, and finished in the best manner.

155.—*Victoria Phaeton.* For one or two horses; on loops; without top; with rumble that can be changed to a dickey seat in front; splash fenders back and front; spring back and cushion; finished in the finest manner in every part. For fair weather there is nothing more comfortable.

156.—*Loop Victoria.* With dickey seat and rumble, both of which can be removed; pole and shafts; back splash fenders; front fenders and dash in one piece, giving a superior finish; spring back and cushions; trimmed and ironed in the most expensive manner; in fact, making one of the most comfortable as well as gorgeous looking Carriages.

No. 157.—C *Spring Victoria.* Medium size, for one or two horses; with seat on hinges for two children; splash fenders back and front; spring back and cushion; finished in the best possible manner. The combination of C and elliptic springs without perch is entirely new, and, for aught we know, originated with us. It is certain, however, that it surpasses all other combinations for lightness and ease.

158.—*Victoria.* Medium size; same in every respect as No. 157, with the exception of C springs.

159.—*Victoria.* Full size; splash fenders back and front; seat on hinges for two children; trimmed with the best of goods, and finished in the richest manner throughout.

160.—*Victoria.* With rumble behind; otherwise same as No. 159.

161.—*Victoria.* On loops; same as No. 156, except that it has no rumble.

162.—*Six-Seat Beach Wagon.* The middle seat can be reversed, so that four persons can face each other, or it can be entirely removed; finished plain but rich. It is decidedly a most sensible Wagon for fair weather, and very light for two horses.

☞ We make this same Wagon with a top on the back seat and doors in the sides.

163.—*Siamese Phaeton.* With movable rumble; without perch; imitation cane seats; splash arm fenders and

a storm apron. This is a new, light, convenient, and most elegant no-top Carriage, finished in the best manner.

164.—*Fine Six-Seat Rockaway.* Scroll back quarters; shifting front quarters; partition front with two drop lights; high doors; stationary lights in back quarters; footman stand; no perch; hangs low, which is very desirable, but not common, in a six-seat Rockaway; spring back and cushions; spring curtains; finished, in every respect, in the best style.

165.—*National Rockaway.* For six persons; without perch; front curtain making it perfectly close for four persons. A footman stand, or baggage rack, can be put on if required. Usually trimmed with cloth or leather. This is one of the most roomy, yet lightest Rockaways, without perch, that can be made. For a plain article nothing is more fashionable.

166.—*National Rockaway.* With perch; otherwise same as No. 165.

167.—*Six-Seat Rockaway.* Full swept; no perch; drop lights in back and back quarters; curtain front quarters; partition front with two drop lights; opera board; spring curtains; usually finished plain but nice. A most comfortable and durable Carriage.

168.—*Six-Seat Paneled Rockaway.* Drop light in back quarters; shifting glass front quarters; partition front with drop light; hung on perch with three springs; footman stand; well plated, and made showy throughout.

169.—*Light Curtain Rockaway.* For six persons; on perch, with two springs; footman stand; usually trimmed with cloth or leather. A very light and tasty Carriage.

170.—*Full-Swept Six-Seat Rockaway.* On perch; with curtains in back quarters; otherwise same as No. 167.

171.—*Six-Seat Ambulance.* The back to front seat is so arranged that it can be taken out and placed between the front and back seats, making a very comfortable bed; shifting baggage rack. A very light Carriage for two horses.

172.—*Light, Open, Five-Seat Rockaway.* For one or two horses; front curtain; front seat made to take out; turn up foot-board. A very convenient Carriage.

173.—*Skeleton Six-Seat Rockaway.* For one or two horses. The front seat is on hinges, and drops out of the way. The middle seat is movable several inches, to accommodate the front seat, or can be taken entirely out. A curtain knobs on the door frame, making quite a close Carriage. This is one of the lightest six-seat standing tops.

174.—*American Six-Seat Phaeton.* An entirely new article; with carved sides, but can be finished plain; storm boot. Made throughout in the very best manner; and, for beauty of style, equal to anything of the kind.

175.—*German Six-Seat Phaeton.* Carved panels, but can be finished plain; carved back bar; storm boot; usually trimmed with leather. or worsted reps, and finished in first class style.

176.—*Central Park Phaeton.* With carved sides, but can be finished plain; shifting seats and top, producing three different styles. This is decidedly a light, roomy, and stylish Carriage, and will give entire satisfaction.

177.—*American Phaeton.* Plain sides; carved seats, with round corners; spring back and cushion; finished plain and rich.

178.—*French Phaeton.* Carved panels; plain seats, with round corners; seats and top can be made to shift if required; finished in the best manner, and is a beautiful article.

179.—*King Phaeton.* Plain sides and seats, cane panel in front; spring back and cushion. This is a large, roomy, comfortable, strong, and very rich-looking Carriage in the street.

180.—*English Square Phaeton.* Shifting top if required; very plain, but well finished. A most beautiful Carriage, light, but yet with plenty of room.

181.—*Light Yacht Phaeton.* Carved panels; seats with round corners; roll-up shifting top; for one or two horses. This is of the very best material, and can be made very light, *i.e.*, 425 lbs.; and for room and beauty is not to be excelled. No. 191 will show it without top, and plain panels; No. 213 with full top.

182.—*Shifting Seat Box Wagon.* For one or two horses. Roll-up and shifting top; both seats can be taken entirely out.

183.—*Shifting Seat Phaeton.* On perch; for one or two horses. A very light and beautiful article, finished with the very best material throughout.

SLEIGHS.

184.—*Albany Cutter.* Trimmed with either plush or carpet; strong and beautifully painted.

185.—*Light Two-Seat Sleigh.* The front seat turns forward or can be taken out. A very nice Sleigh for one or two horses; finished in the best manner.

186.—*Fine Pony Sleigh.* Beautifully painted and trimmed; made for service.

265.—*Portland Sleigh.* Carved body; made very

light; ironed, plated, painted, and trimmed in the most expensive manner.

☞ We can furnish larger Sleighs, with or without tops; also any size and pattern, trimmed or untrimmed, of almost any price, at short notice.

187.—*French Dog Cart.* Without perch; carved panels; back end hung on hinges and chains; lazy back on hinges, so that persons can sit facing either way; back seat hung on hinges, and made to turn forward into the body and fasten with a lock. The end lid closes, and is also fastened with a lock. Finished in the very best manner, and can be made either showy or plain.

188.—*American Dog Cart.* On double perch, for one or two horses; carved back panels and seat; back seat on hinges, and, when closed, is not seen; large closed box under front seat; finished with the very best material, and can be made light or heavy. A perfect gem.

189.—*Shifting-Seat Box Wagon.* On perch, for one or two horses; wheels to run under. The peculiarity of this Wagon is, the back seat is so arranged, that there is as much room as a larger body affords; and when the seat is taken off from the body and spring bar, by two screws, there is a well-proportioned body for one seat. The front seat can be moved back several inches, or entirely removed.

190.—*Light Box Wagon.* Same as No. 189, except the cut-under and height of front seat. It is also of less weight. Both are finished equal to the very best made Wagons.

191.—*American Yacht Wagon.* Round-cornered seats with bent wood wings; hung on double perch; can be finished with carved panels and half-top, same as No. 181, or as No. 213. For room, beauty, lightness, and finish it has no superior.

192.—*Clipper Wagon.* On double perch; swelled sides and back panel; round-cornered seats; finished in the best manner; and can be made as light as a Wagon for four persons ever should be.

193.—*Popular Wagon.* Plain sides; round-cornered seats, with wood wings; body usually painted plain, and running part fancy.

194.—*York Wagon.* Plain sides; seats with solid round corners, and wood wings extending around the seat; back seat can be taken off; usually trimmed with leather or reps; finished in the best possible manner. A Wagon that is never out of style.

195.—*Cut-under Turn-Out-Seat Buggie.* Back seat on hinges. This is a rather expensive body, the front pillars and seat corners being worked out of solid wood; leather wings to seat, the whole finished with the very best material. Can be finished with a top like No. 261.

196.—*Sensible Buggie, with Turn-Out Seat.* This is a very light article for four persons, and is beautifully finished in every particular. It can be made with top like Nos. 285 or 293.

197.—*Turn-Out Seat Buggie.* Back seat on hinges. Can be finished with top like No. 264. Made strong and substantial.

198.—*Drop-Front Buggie.* With turn-out seat; lazy back can be taken off. Can be finished with close or roll-up top, as No. 263. Strong and durable.

199.—*French Jump Seat.* Plated rail on back seat instead of a top. Is adjusted from a two to a one seat, same as No. 283.

200.—*Six-Seat Chariotee.* A roomy substantial Carriage, made either showy or plain.

201.—*Unique Chariotee.* A new pattern; with leather or wood dash; turn-up footman stand; is very roomy, and can be finished with light or heavy running part. Usually showy, and trimmed with leather.

202.—*Slide-Seat No-Top Buggie.* Box body; strong and substantial throughout. Can be finished with top, same as No. 255.

203.—*Slide-Seat No-Top Buggie.* Same as Nos. 250 and 251, except top.

204.—*Carved Chariotee.* Made strong and generally showy.

205.—*English Chariotee.* New style; revolving backs; footman stand; can be made showy or plain, and hung on light or heavy Carriage part. Warranted to give satisfaction.

206.—*Wide-World No-Top Buggie.* Usually finished plain, and made for service.

207.—*Cut-under No-Top Buggie.* Plated rail and braces; open back; or finished with turn-out seat similar to No. 198; turns short; made strong.

208.—*Crane-Neck Chariotee.* Scroll back quarters, and carved neck; revolving backs; turn-up footman stand; usually well plated and finished rather showy. A nice, roomy, strong, and substantial Carriage.

209.—*Cabriolet Chariotee.* For one or two horses; made of the very best material throughout; finished plain, but rich. This is a very light and graceful Carriage; weighing about 500 lbs.; finished with close, gipsy, or full roll-up top; or, like No. 153, with half top;

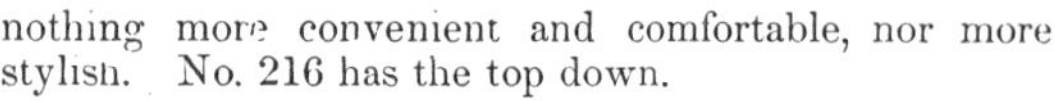

nothing more convenient and comfortable, nor more stylish. No. 216 has the top down.

210.—*Plantation No-Top Buggie.* Roomy, strong, convenient, as well as cheap.

211.—*Antique No-Top Buggie.* Crooked body; solid seat; wood dash; iron rack. Good, plain, and low priced. No. 249 shows it with top.

212.—*French Chariotee.* Carved panels; gipsey top; can be finished with plain panels, and with either close or roll-up top; made of the best material; and is a beautiful and comfortable Carriage.

213.—*American Yacht Shifting-Top Chariotee.* Carved panels; finished plain and without top, would be like No. 191. The body of this is made very strong, with but little iron; the whole Carriage weighs only from 400 to 450 lbs. For room, beauty, strength, and lightness, it has no superior.

214.—*Sensible No-Top Buggie.* Heavy front pillars; carved seat, and solid round seat corners; leather wings; usually finished plain, but very rich. This is a Buggie made for hard service; of the very best material in every particular; weighing from 250 to 300 lbs. It will not dishonor its name. No. 285 shows it with close top, and No. 293 with roll-up top, and plain seat panels.

215.—*Excelsior Trotter.* On elliptic springs; sides and back swelled; round-cornered seat, and wood wings worked in solid; homogeneous steel tire and axles; beautifully trimmed and painted; weighing only from 200 to 235 lbs. We will simply remark here, that the manufacturing world can produce nothing superior to our light work in style, beauty of finish, and strength. No. 291 represents it with a beautiful roll-up top.

216.—*Light Cabriolet Chariotee.* Top down; for description of which see No. 209, which has the top up.

217.—*Every Day No-Top Buggie.*—Weighs from 225 to 250 lbs.; made of the very best material in all its parts; body all wood, and made in the most approved manner; beautifully painted and trimmed, and is what it purports to be, *i. e*, a serviceable every-day Buggie. No. 290 shows it with solid seat and roll-up top.

218.—*English Brougham Rockaway.* Without perch; full size; drop lights in back quarters, which can be finished with stationary oval lights, like No. 226, or close paneled like No. 219; swelled back; partition front with two drop lights; extra revolving backs, to use when partition is removed; spring back and cushion; spring curtains; usually trimmed with cloth or silk inside, and leather front. Elegantly finished throughout.

219.—*American Sociable Rockaway.* Close back quarters, but can be finished with drop lights, like No. 218, or stationary, like No. 226. The bottom of doors are concaved. and extend to bottom of body—something entirely new, and makes a most beautiful Carriage. In other respects it is similar to No. 218.

220.—*York Wagon.* Single seat; body usually painted plain, and running part handsomely striped; is of medium weight, and made of the best materials, for real service.

221.—*Skeleton Wagon.* Made to weigh from 75 to 135 lbs.

222.—*Light Curtain Sociable Rockaway.* Revolving backs, but can be finished with a movable partition front, making it close for two persons; bottom of doors concaved to bottom of body. This is a very roomy, light, and graceful Carriage, and the most elegant Curtain Rockaway we have ever made; finished in the most superior manner throughout.

223.—*Brougham Rockaway.* Paneled back, with drop light; spring curtains; revolving backs to front seat; footman stand and holders; of medium size and weight; made for service. Can be finished with movable partition front and close panel, or with drop or stationary lights in back quarters.

224.—*Light Box No-Top Buggie.* With stick seat; made either light or heavy, plain or showy. A good, sensible Wagon.

225.—*Pony Buggie.* For Children. Carved seat; leather wings; made in the most perfect manner throughout.

226.—*American Sociable Rockaway.* On perch, for one or two horses; stationary lights in back quarters, but can be made with drop lights, like No. 218, or close, like No. 219; movable partition front, with drop lights; extra revolving backs, when partition is removed; bottom of doors concaved. The whole is finished in a most beautiful manner, presenting one of the most elegant Rockaways made.

227.—*O G Turn-over Seat Rockaway.* For one or two horses; made very light, but for service; front seat on hinges, and turns forward; usually trimmed with leather or cloth.

228.—*Georgia No-Top Buggie.* Side springs; can be finished plain or showy. A good and strong, cheap and comfortable Buggie.

229.—*Legion No-Top Buggie.* Movable back and rack; boot creased, stitched, striped, or moulded; can be finished plain or showy, and is made for service.

230.—*Light Columbian Rockaway.* On perch, for one or two horses; revolving backs; opera board; drop lights in back quarters, with stationary glass top and bottom; can be finished with one stationary light, or with a curtain, also with partition front. This is a light,

roomy, and beautiful little Carriage, and made for service.

231.—*Four-Seat Germantown Rockaway.* Front seat to turn forward; footman stand; light, strong, and serviceable.

232.—*Concord No-Top Buggie.* Side springs; creased or stitched boot; usually made rather plain, but of the best material, and for real service. This Buggie is in almost universal use.

233.—*Medium No-Top Buggie.* Wood dash; leather boot; paneled seat; strong, comfortable, and cheap.

234.—*Scroll Four-Seat Curtain Rockaway.* For one or two horses; turn down footman stand; revolving backs, but can be finished with partition front; or with drop lights in back quarters like No. 218; is very roomy, and usually trimmed with cloth or leather, and finished for durability.

235.—*Compass Four-Seat Curtain Rockaway.* Footman stand; curtains that knob on, and open with the doors; generally trimmed with leather; can be finished plain or showy. A light, roomy, and desirable little Carriage.

236.—*Tilbury No-Top Buggie.* Movable back and rack; wood dash; made showy or plain. A strong and durable article, with plenty of seat and foot room, and will give general satisfaction.

237.—*Philadelphia No-Top Buggie.* Paneled sides; nicely ornamented; light, roomy, and made for real service.

238.—*Light Eureka, Turn-out Seat, Curtain Rockaway.* Bottom panels concaved; elegantly trimmed and painted; very roomy, and yet only weighing from 450 to 500 lbs. This is something entirely new, and the Carriage itself must be seen to be fully appreciated.

239.—*Light No-Top Business Wagon.* On half springs, but can be hung on full elliptics; seat on spring bars, which affords additional ease, and can be taken out; weighs from 200 to 225 lbs.; made of the best stock, and will "stand."

240.—*Movable Top Jagger Wagon.* Leather curtains; generally trimmed with leather; one or both seats can be moved, or taken out; top takes off, thus combining three or four styles in one. In fact this is one of the lightest, most convenient, and best finished Wagons, and not very expensive.

241.—*Beauty, No-Top Trotter.*—Side and back panels swelled; round-cornered seat, with solid wood wings; hung on wood spring bars and half springs; axles and tires of homogeneous steel. There is nothing put into any of its parts but the very best material known. It combines lightness with its strength, weighing only from 150 to 175 lbs. For beauty of style, finish, lightness, and durability, it is conceded by every Carriage connoisseur, to have no competitor.

242.—*Handsome, No-Top Trotter.* This Trotter differs from No. 241, in that the body is hung upon half elliptic side springs, instead of being bolted directly to the spring bars; the seat has no wings; it is also from five to ten pounds lighter than No. 241; in all other respects precisely similar. Two handsomer, more stylish, or better made Trotters, never appeared upon a race course.

243.—*Quinnipiack Jump Seat Rockaway.* Made light, suitable for one or two horses; seats with high and full backs; neatly finished throughout. No 246 shows it in the two-seat form.

244.—*Continental Top Buggie.* Wood dash; high, full back; shifting rack; good, strong, and cheap.

245.—*Shifting Top Tilbury.* Wood dash; shifting rack; nicely painted, and made for durability. A fine-looking Buggie with or without top. Can be finished like No. 236, or No. 256.

246.—*Quinnipiack Jump Seat Rockaway.* In a two-seat form; same as No. 243.

247.—*Jump Seat Top Wagon.* Very light; for one horse; made for service and cheap.

248.—*Prince Albert Buggie.* Roll up top; high, full back; leather dash; shifting rack; nicely finished throughout, will do first-rate service, and is cheap. No. 282 presents it with a wood dash, close top, and wheels to run under.

249.—*Antique Buggie.* Roll up shifting top; iron rack; wood dash; well plated; strong and comfortable. No. 211 shows it without top.

250.—*Slide Seat Buggie.* Crooked body; wood dash; gipsy top; rack; high full back; very roomy and durable; made either showy or plain. It requires but a moment to change it into a one-seat form, same as No. 251, and is like that, with the exception of the full top, or like No. 203 without top, presenting a beautiful one-seat Buggie.

251.—*Closed Extension Top Slide Seat Buggie.* Same as No. 250, with the exception of the top. No 254 shows it in a two-seat form. For a light, shifting-seat article, for one or two horses, there is nothing superior.

252.—*Cash Buggie.* Crooked body; roll up top; high back; open lid, or can be made with a turn-out seat, similar to No. 198, with but little extra expense; making a good, desirable Buggie, at the lowest possible price.

No. 253.—*Concord Top Buggie.* Finished either plain or showy; a comfortable and very cheap Buggie.

254.—*Open Extension Top Slide Seat.* In two-seat form. No. 251 shows it in a one-seat form, No. 203 without top, and No. 250 with half top, and gives a full description.

255.—*Box Slide-Seat Buggie.* Light and roomy; the easiest adjusted, and one of the most desirable of Slide Seats; made either showy or plain, and for service. No. 202 is the same without top, and in a closed form.

256.—*Tilbury Buggie.* Gipsy top; wood dash; shifting rack; finished either showy or plain; or like No. 245. Turns short; is of medium weight; will do excelent service; nothing more comfortable or better for the money.

257.—*Universal Box-Buggie.* Full back; roll-up top; of medium weight; comfortable, roomy, and the cheapest Box-Buggie extant.

258.—*Turn-Out Seat Box-Buggie.* Made strong and for service. A very convenient and easy Carriage.

259.—*Shifting-Top Turn-Out-Seat Buggie.* Wheels to run under; carved wood in back panels; made either showy or plain. There is no lighter Carriage for four persons.

260.—*Park Phaeton.* Roll-up top, spring joints; full plated; finely painted and ornamented; easy to get in and out of, and a very comfortable Carriage.

261.—*Cut-Under Buggie.*—For one or two horses; close top; back box with lid to lock, but can be made with a turn-out seat, similar to No. 195; spring cushion and back; usually made plain, but of the very best material. This is one of the richest, most comfortable, as well as most expensive Buggies made.

262.—*Doctor's Heavy Phaeton.* With rumble, hood, and side lights; spring joints, and lamps; generally trimmed with black leather; patent coupling allowing the wheels to run under body; made very roomy and strong for constant use. No. 281 shows it without rumble.

263.—*Drop-Front Turn-Out-Seat Buggie.* With roll-up top and baggage rack; made either showy or plain; convenient, roomy, and strong. No. 198 shows it without top.

264.—*Turn-Out-Seat Buggie.* Straight body; open front; roll-up shifting top. A light, roomy, and very desirable Buggie. No. 197 shows it without top.

265.—*Portland Sleigh.* For description of which see under head of Sleighs. Nos. 184, 185, and 186.

266.—*C Spring Brainard Gig.* Roll-up top; spring joints; spring cushion and back; patent coupling to turn short; made of the very best material in every respect. This is hung on an entirely new principle. For physicians, or those who are constantly riding, there is nothing equal to it for ease or elegance. No. 289 shows the same on elliptic springs, and close top.

267.—*Spanish Prince Albert.* Carved and highly ornamented body; roll-up top; hood; rack; patent coupling, enabling wheels to run under body; usually trimmed with silk goods· full plated; in fact gorgeously finished throughout.

268.—*Eureka Jump-Seat.*—Shown as a Phaeton, or single Buggie; with high back; roll-up top and spring joints. By one motion it can be changed into a two-seat form, as shown in No. 271, producing one of the most elegant of Jump-Seat Buggies. This article can be finished with either wood or leather dash, plain or showy.

269.—*Common-Sense Buggie.* Shifting top; carved seat panels; solid front pillars; made of the very best material, and in the most expensive manner; weighing from 300 to 330 lbs.; elegant with or without top; one of the most sensible Buggies for constant service.

270.—*Doctor's York-Phaeton.* Medium weight; close top; side lights; spring joints; wheels to run under body; spring cushion and back; large apron; roomy; convenient to get in and out of; usually finished plain, but elegant, and for service. Universally used in all large cities.

271.—*Eureka Jump-Seat Buggie.* Two-seat form, otherwise same as No. 268.

272.—*New Orleans Jump-Seat Buggie.* Wood dash; crooked body; shifting top; spring joints; hood; full plated; made showy, and meets with general favor. No. 275 shows the same in a one-seat form.

273. *Standing-Top Doctor's Phaeton.* Crooked body; wood dash; skeleton door; side curtains to knob on the doors; patent short coupling. This is one of the closest, most convenient, and comfortable Phaetons for physicians' use. Usually trimmed with leather and made plain for service.

274.—*Gazelle Cut-under Buggie.* Roll-up top; movable rack; wood dash; high back; wheels, though high, will run under body; is of medium weight, and usually made rather showy; a very graceful, roomy, and most desirable Buggie.

275.—*New Orleans Jump-Seat Buggie.* Closed; in a one-seat form; otherwise same as No. 272.

276.—*Extension Top Jump-Seat Buggie.* A new style of shifting top, which requires but a moment to change;

finished either showy or plain. No. 279 shows it in a two-seat form.

277.—*Light Shifting-Top Box-Buggie.* Creased and stiched boot; weighs from 300 to 350 lbs.; is made for hard service, such as Livery or constant business use; roomy, comfortable, and fine looking with or without top.

278.—*Queen's Phaeton.* Gipsy top, but can be finished with close or roll-up top; high back, and roomy both in width and length; hangs low, and is easy of access, being peculiarly adapted for either old or infirm people. For ease, style, and comfort, it cannot be excelled.

279.—*Extension Top-Jump-Seat Buggie.* Open, in a two-seat form; otherwise same as No. 276.

280.—*Box Jump-Seat Buggie.* Open, in a two-seat form; shifting roll-up top, spring joints; finished either showy or plain. This is the lightest, most comfortable, and popular Jump-Seat ever invented. No. 283 presents it in a one-seat form, and No. 199 without a top.

281.—*Full-Size Phaeton.* Same as No. 262, except having no rumble.

282.—*English Prince Albert.* Wood dash; shifting rack; close top; side lights; hood; lamps; easy of access; exceedingly roomy and comfortable; usually finished plain, but neat and substantial; can be made very showy. No 248 shows it with leather dash, roll-up top, and high front-wheels. A most desirable and cheap Buggie.

283.—*Box Jump-Seat Buggie.* Closed; in a one-seat form; in other respects same as No. 280.

284.—*Draw-Front Phaeton.* Closed; high back; close top and spring joints; lamps; wheels run under body; usually trimmed with black leather; finished plain but fine; made of the best and most durable material throughout. This is the most convenient and roomy shifting-seat made; is adjusted in a moment, and has a fine appearance, either in a closed, or, as No. 287, in an open form.

285.—*Sensible Buggie.* Shifting close-top; high back; weighs from 300 to 350 lbs.; otherwise same as No. 214. No. 293 presents it with a roll-up top, and plain panels to seat. No better Buggie is made.

286.—*Deep Side-Box-Buggie.* Close-top, spring joints; high back and arms; very roomy; hung low; made of the best material. There is nothing superior for richness of style, comfort, and durability. Weighs from 335 to 375 lbs.

287.—*Draw-Front Phaeton.* Open, otherwise same as No. 284.

288.—*Superior Top-Buggie.* Finished similar to No. 286, but has a lighter appearance, and weighs from 35 to 50 lbs. less. A most beautiful Buggie.

289.—*Light Brainard Gig.* Close top; side lights; spring joints; spring back and cushion; patent turn short; weighs from 300 to 350 lbs. No. 266 shows it on C springs, and with roll-up top; usually finished plain, but for style, richness of finish, quality of material, ease of access, and luxurious comfort, these two are incomparable.

290.—*Every-Day Buggie.* Shifting roll-up top; body all wood; made so as to combine great strength with little weight; as for quality of material, there can be nothing superior made use of in a Buggie; body usually finished plain, and Carriage part a little showy. This is a most elegant and substantial Buggie, and weighs from 285 to 315 lbs. No 217 shows it with stick seat, and no top.

291.—*Excelsior Trotter.* With roll-up top that takes off from under cushion, leaving the seat free from all projecting irons; bows, joints, top, and dash irons, all covered and wound; weighs from 250 to 300 lbs. This has been pronounced superior to anything in market, for lightness, durability, beauty of style, and finish. For further particulars see No. 215

292.—*Hunting Wagon.* Close top, spring joints; high, full back; extra leather boot to close body back of seat; finished plain; of the best material, and is of medium weight. For hunting and carrying packages, etc., there is no Wagon more appropriate.

293.—*Sensible Buggie.* With roll-up shifting top, and plain seat panels; otherwise same as Nos. 214 and 285.

294.—*Road Sulky.* We can furnish Sulkies either light or heavy, well or inferior made, showy or plain, and of any form desired.

295.—*Boston Chaise.* Roll-up top; lancewood shafts; high spring back; made for service; usually finished plain but nice.

296.—*Stanhope.* Hung on either painted or plated loops; creased or stitched boot; lamps; step standard; made light and fancy.

297.—*Light French Dog-Cart.* Hung on half springs, and two wheels. The back seat, when not in use, can be turned up so as to form a back to front seat; sides finished with either real or imitation blinds. One of the lightest and most desirable Dog Carts.

298.—*Barnsbury Cart.* On half and cross springs; back seat slides; the body can be made stationary or movable, for the purpose of balancing, as the weight to be carried may require. It is a light, roomy, and most comfortable Cart; and can be finished very showy, or plain.

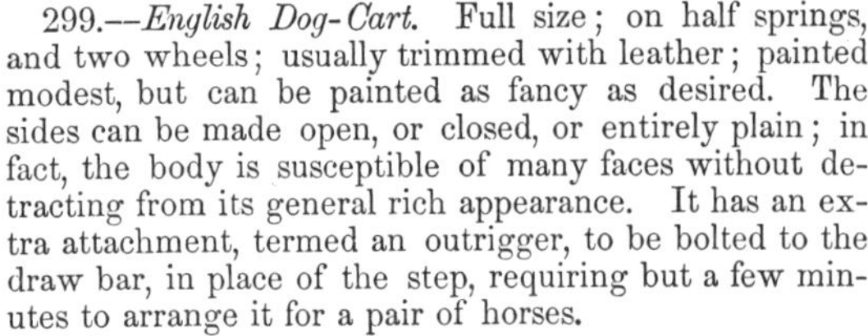

299.—*English Dog-Cart.* Full size; on half springs, and two wheels; usually trimmed with leather; painted modest, but can be painted as fancy as desired. The sides can be made open, or closed, or entirely plain; in fact, the body is susceptible of many faces without detracting from its general rich appearance. It has an extra attachment, termed an outrigger, to be bolted to the draw bar, in place of the step, requiring but a few minutes to arrange it for a pair of horses.

300.—*Shamrock Cart.* On half springs and two wheels; panels of carved wood, but can be finished plain. This is exceedingly roomy, both in width and length; and yet made in such a manner as to be unusually light. The whole appearance is elegant, and it is a great favorite with sporting gentlemen.

301.—*Bombay Chaise.* With step; very roomy and comfortable; usually finished plain, but nice; strong, and for service.

302.—*Bombay Chaise.* With rumble instead of step; otherwise same as No. 301.

303.—*Step Chaise.* On half and cross elliptic springs; roll-up top; hood; spring back; full plate; lamps, etc.; finished most elegantly, and of the best material; can be made plain and rich, and without the step; nothing superior in the Chaise line.

HARNESS.—See p. 44.

We have devoted but one page to Harness, for the reason that the general outlines of a Harness, on paper, vary but little, while in reality there must necessarily be a wide difference in the quality of the material used, as well as in the amount of labor expended. For instance Single Harness vary in price from $10 to $100, and Double Harness from $20 to $200.

1. Light Shifting Harness.
2. Heavy Coach do.
3. Fine Single do.
4. Plain do. do.

Whips from 50 cents to $10.

In ordering Harness please state whether you wish light or heavy; plain or showy; the color of the stitching; the plate; and also the price. We will use our best endeavors to give perfect satisfaction to all who may favor us with their orders.

SADDLES.

Saddles also vary so little in their general appearance on paper, that we have thought it worth while to present but a few engravings. The illustrations given convey a very correct idea of the peculiar style of each.

We can furnish any kind of Saddles that may be required, of any quality, and in any quantity; also Bridles, Martingales, etc.

1. San Antonio Saddle.
2. Spanish Horn do.
3. Smith do.
4. Fine Leaping Horn Side-Saddle.

} See page 64.

5. English Saddle with cloth.
6. Straight Head Saddle.
7. Common Side-Saddle.
8. Spanish, no Horn do.

} See page 78.

9. McClellan's Saddle.
10. Dragoon Saddle.
11. Half Hussar Saddle.
12. Leaping Horn Side-Saddle.

} See page 125.

PRICE LIST.

Payable in gold or its equivalent

CARRIAGES.

NO.	FROM $	TO $	NO.	FROM $	TO $	NO.	FROM $	TO $	NO.	FROM $	TO $	NO.	FROM $	TO $	NO.	FROM $	TO $	NO.	FROM $	TO $
101	1250	1500	130	850	950	159	525	650	188	275	325	217	125	150	246	225	275	275	200	250
102	750	1000	131	750	850	160	600	650	189	250	275	218	500	600	247	150	200	276	200	250
103	900	1100	132	650	750	161	650	750	190	225	250	219	475	550	248	145	175	277	165	185
104	1250	1500	133	625	725	162	275	325	191	225	250	220	135	150	249	135	170	278	165	225
105	750	900	134	800	1000	163	350	400	192	200	225	221	80	95	250	150	175	279	200	250
106	750	1000	135	700	900	164	650	750	193	200	250	222	350	400	251	175	200	280	185	235
107	950	1100	136	750	850	165	450	500	194	225	250	223	275	325	252	100	125	281	225	250
108	1000	1100	137	725	825	166	400	450	195	225	250	224	100	150	253	100	135	282	175	200
109	800	1000	138	650	750	167	500	600	196	200	225	225	140	160	254	175	200	283	185	235
110	900	1050	139	600	700	168	400	500	197	125	150	226	350	425	255	150	200	284	250	300
111	800	1000	140	525	650	169	300	375	198	125	150	227	250	300	256	150	185	285	225	275
112	800	1000	141	600	700	170	400	500	199	160	200	228	80	100	257	130	150	286	200	250
113	850	1000	142	650	750	171	250	300	200	400	475	229	100	135	258	150	200	287	250	300
114	550	700	143	600	750	172	270	320	201	300	335	230	325	350	259	150	175	288	225	275
115	500	700	144	500	600	173	225	275	202	125	150	231	220	275	260	200	225	289	225	265
116	700	825	145	550	700	174	500	600	203	125	160	232	75	135	261	250	300	290	215	250
117	600	750	146	500	550	175	475	550	204	275	300	233	95	125	262	250	300	291	235	275
118	600	750	147	500	600	176	400	450	205	250	275	234	300	350	263	155	185	292	225	250
119	600	700	148	475	525	177	400	450	206	115	140	235	200	250	264	165	200	293	225	250
120	600	675	149	475	525	178	400	450	207	95	130	236	110	125	265	100	135	294	75	95
121	90	125	150	375	425	179	450	500	208	300	325	237	110	135	266	235	275	295	200	250
122	50	75	151	325	375	180	425	475	209	325	375	238	275	300	267	175	225	296	150	200
123	475	700	152	300	350	181	315	345	210	85	115	239	125	150	268	250	300	297	200	275
124	10	25	153	320	375	182	275	300	211	95	125	240	200	225	269	225	275	298	275	350
125	500	650	154	350	425	183	350	400	212	325	375	241	135	165	270	235	250	299	325	450
126	500	650	155	450	550	184	75	110	213	315	350	242	135	165	271	250	300	300	300	400
127	8	12	156	650	800	185	80	125	214	140	175	243	225	275	272	200	250	301	250	320
128	1000	1150	157	550	600	186	150	200	215	150	175	244	125	150	273	175	225	302	260	330
129	900	1000	158	500	600	187	400	500	216	325	375	245	140	160	274	150	200	303	240	300

HARNESS.

NO.	DESCRIPTION.	FROM	TO	NO.	DESCRIPTION.	FROM	TO	NO.	DESCRIPTION.	FROM	TO
1	Light Shifting, .	$40	$75	3	Fine Single, . .	$37	$75		Coach Whips, .	$1	$10
2	Heavy Coach, .	65	125	4	Plain Single, . .	18	30		Buggie Whips, .	50c.	8

SADDLES.

NO.	DESCRIPTION.	FROM	TO	NO.	DESCRIPTION.	FROM	TO	NO.	DESCRIPTION.	FROM	TO
1	San Antonio, . .	$18	$24	5	English,	$12	$25	9	M'Clellan's, . .	$15	$18
2	Spanish Horn, .	9	15	6	Straight Head, .	4.50	6.50	10	Dragoon, . .	16	19
3	Smith, ...	20	25	7	Common Side, .	10	15	11	Half Hussar, .	8	11
4	Fine Leaping Horn,	35	40	8	Spanish Horn, .	12	15	12	Leaping Horn,	25	30

New Haven, Conn.

PASSENGER DEPOT, AT NEW HAVEN, CONN.,

OF THE

NEW YORK AND NEW HAVEN RAILROAD COMPANY.

Six Trains daily from New York to New Haven; four Trains daily to Boston—by Shore Line *via* Providence, and inland route *via* Hartford, Springfield, and Worcester; and two Trains *via* Canal Railroad to Northampton — arrive and depart from this Depot.

Fare from New York to New Haven........$1.65. Fare from New York to Boston........$5.00

Depot in New York—Corner of Twenty-seventh Street and Fourth Avenue.

J. R. BUCKLEY, President; **J. H. HOYT**, Superintendent, New York; **E. S. QUINTARD**, Ass't Sup't, New Haven.

NEW HAVEN, HARTFORD AND SPRINGFIELD RAILROAD.

CHAS. F. POND, President. **E. M. REED**, Superintendent.

NEW HAVEN, NEW LONDON AND STONINGTON "SHORE LINE" RAILROAD.

C. S. BUSHNELL, President. **F. J. CALHOUN**, Superintendent.

NEW HAVEN AND NORTHAMPTON COMPANY "CANAL RAILROAD."

WM. JOHNSON, President. **PETER DENNIS**, Sup't. **J. E. SHEFFIELD**, Pres't of Canal Extension.

ILLUSTRATED CATALOGUE.

NEW HAVEN GREEN.

No. 101.

Extra Fine Close Coach.

No. 102.

Medium Size Close Coach.

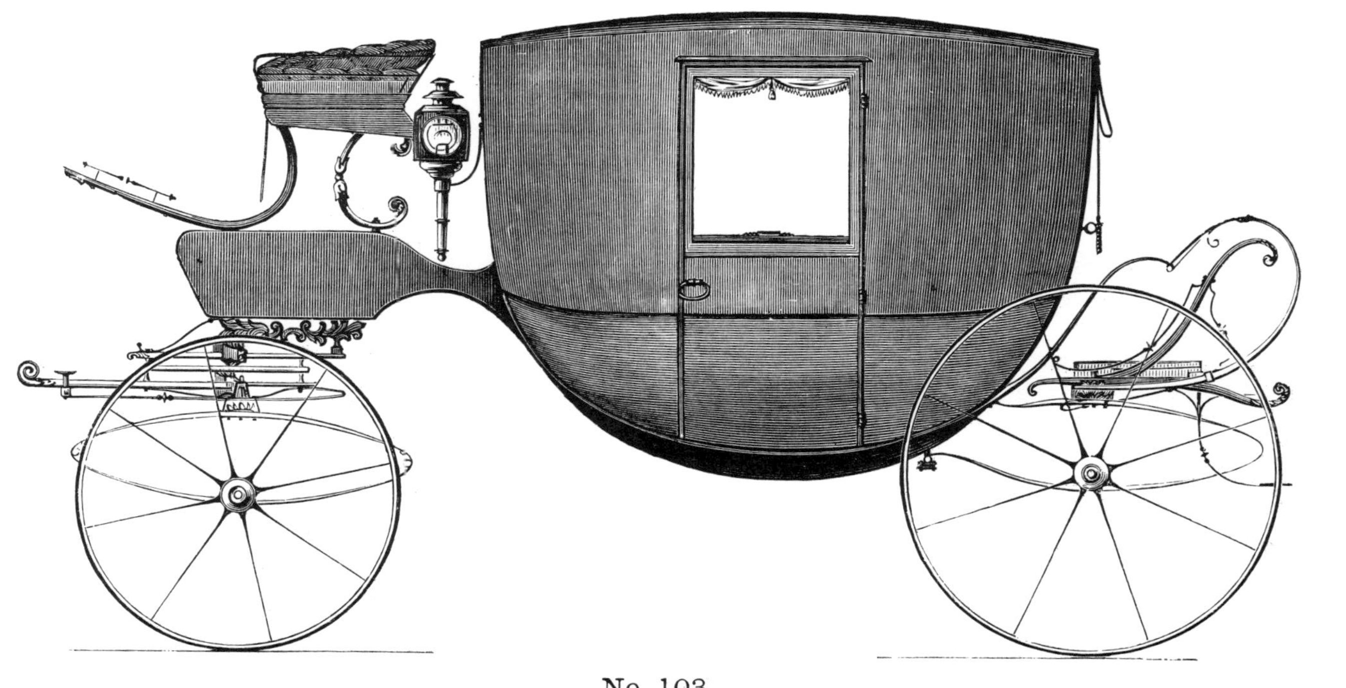

No. 103

Fine Full Size Coach.

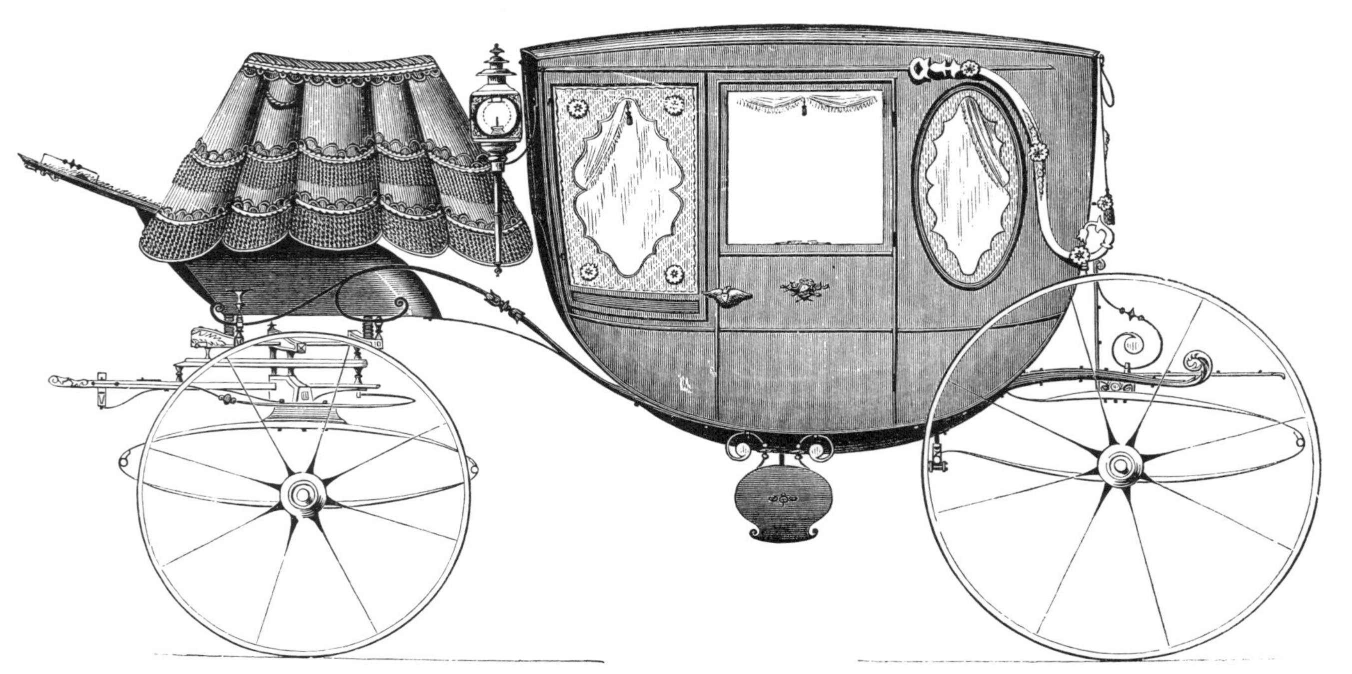

No 104.

A Very Rich Glass-Quartered Coach.

No. 105.

Full Swept Coach.

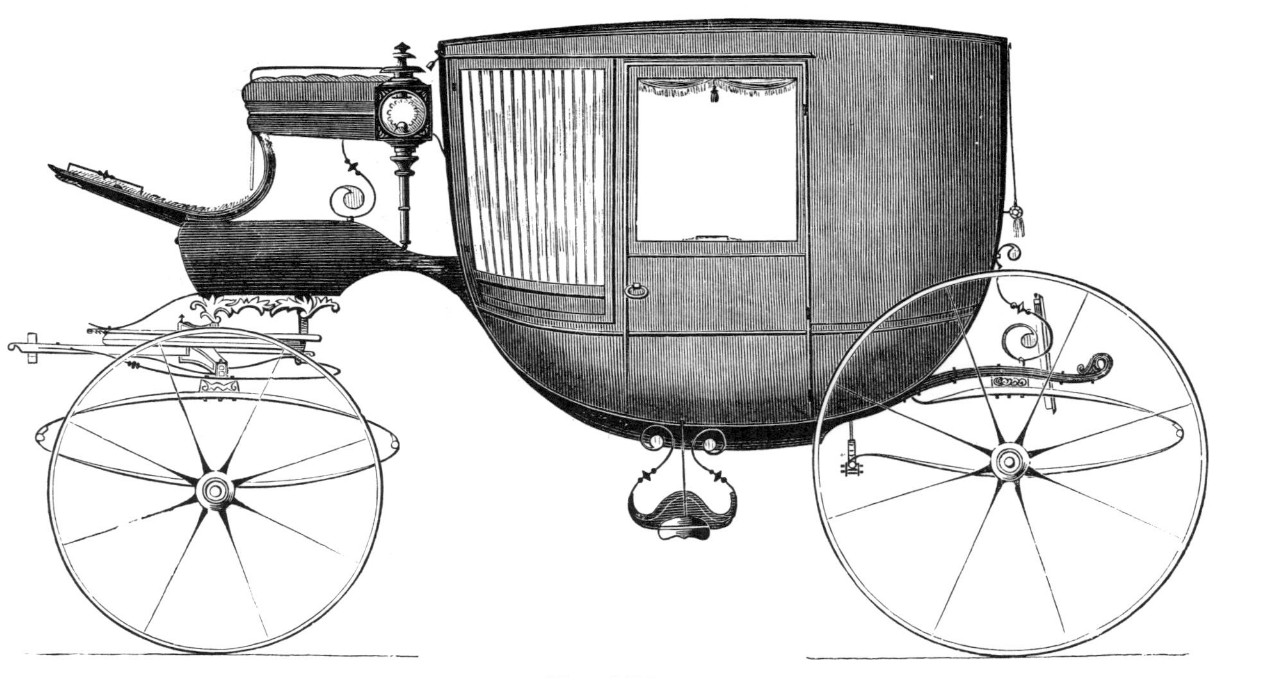

No. 106.

A Close Coach.

No. 107.

Full Size Open Top Coach.

No. 108.

Sociable Caleche Coach.

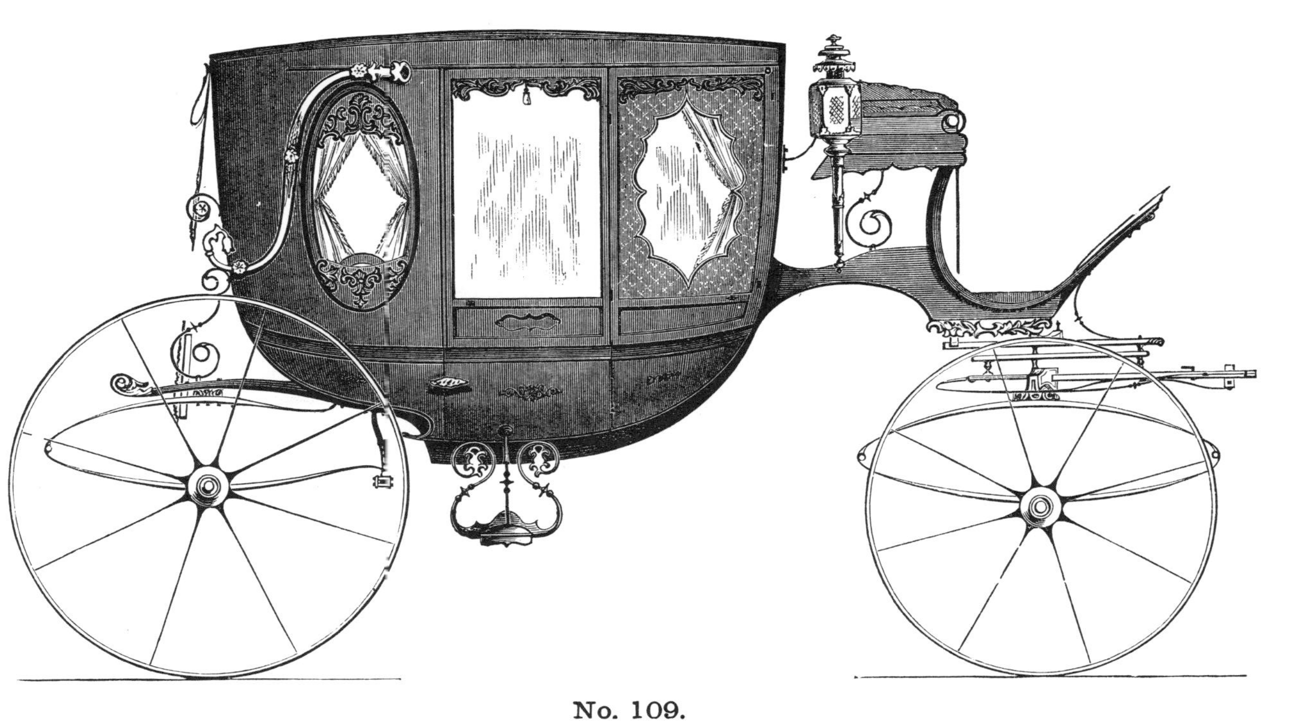

No. 109.

Scroll-Back Quarter Caleche Coach.

No. 110.

Light American Caleche.

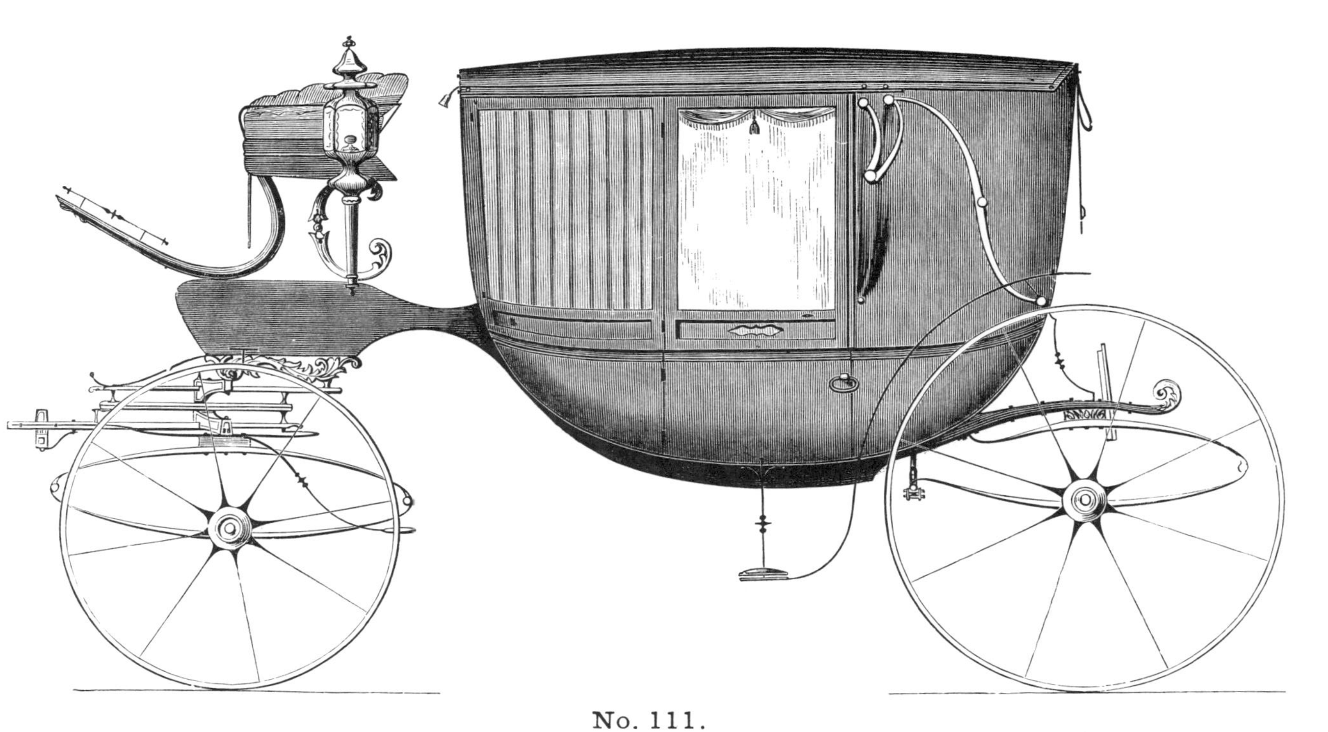

No. 111.

Full Size Round Bottom Caleche.

No. 112.

Light American Caleche.

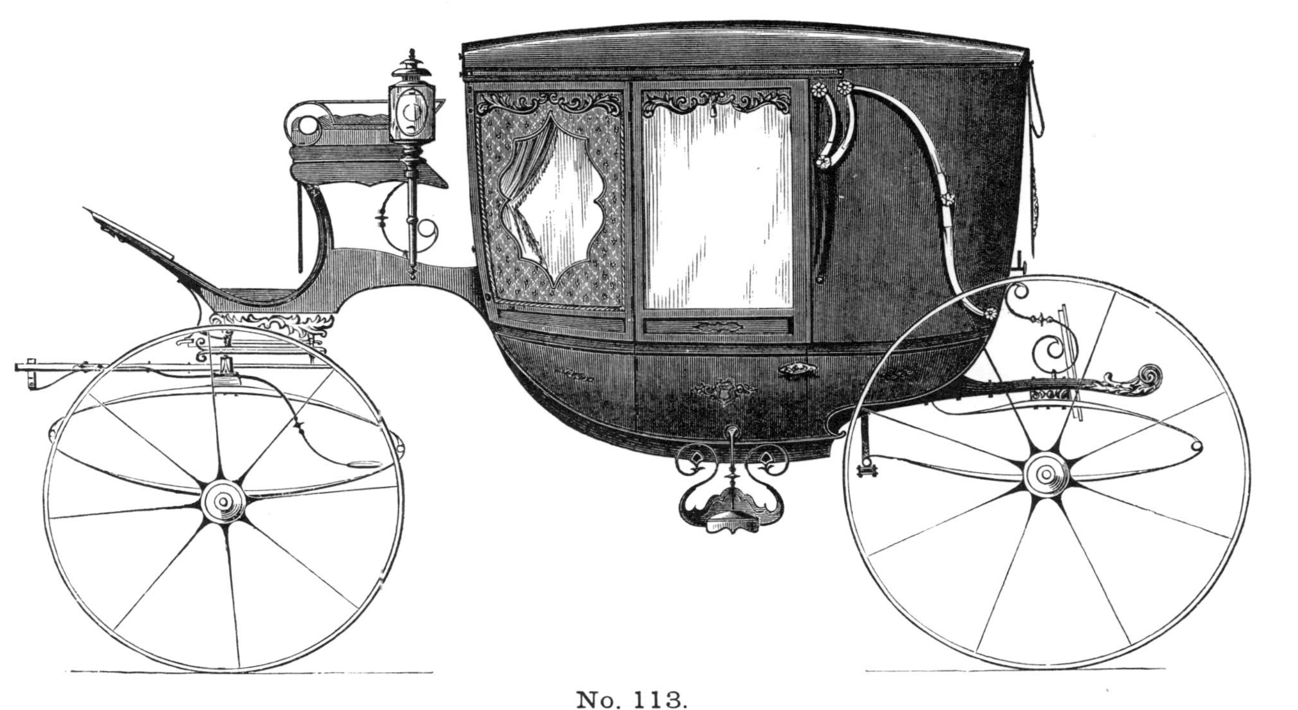

No. 113.

Scroll Back Quarter Caleche.

No. 114.

French Light Curtain Coach.

No. 115.

Curtain Coach.

No. 116.—CRANE NECK CALECHE.

No. 117.—Light Crane Neck Caleche Coach.

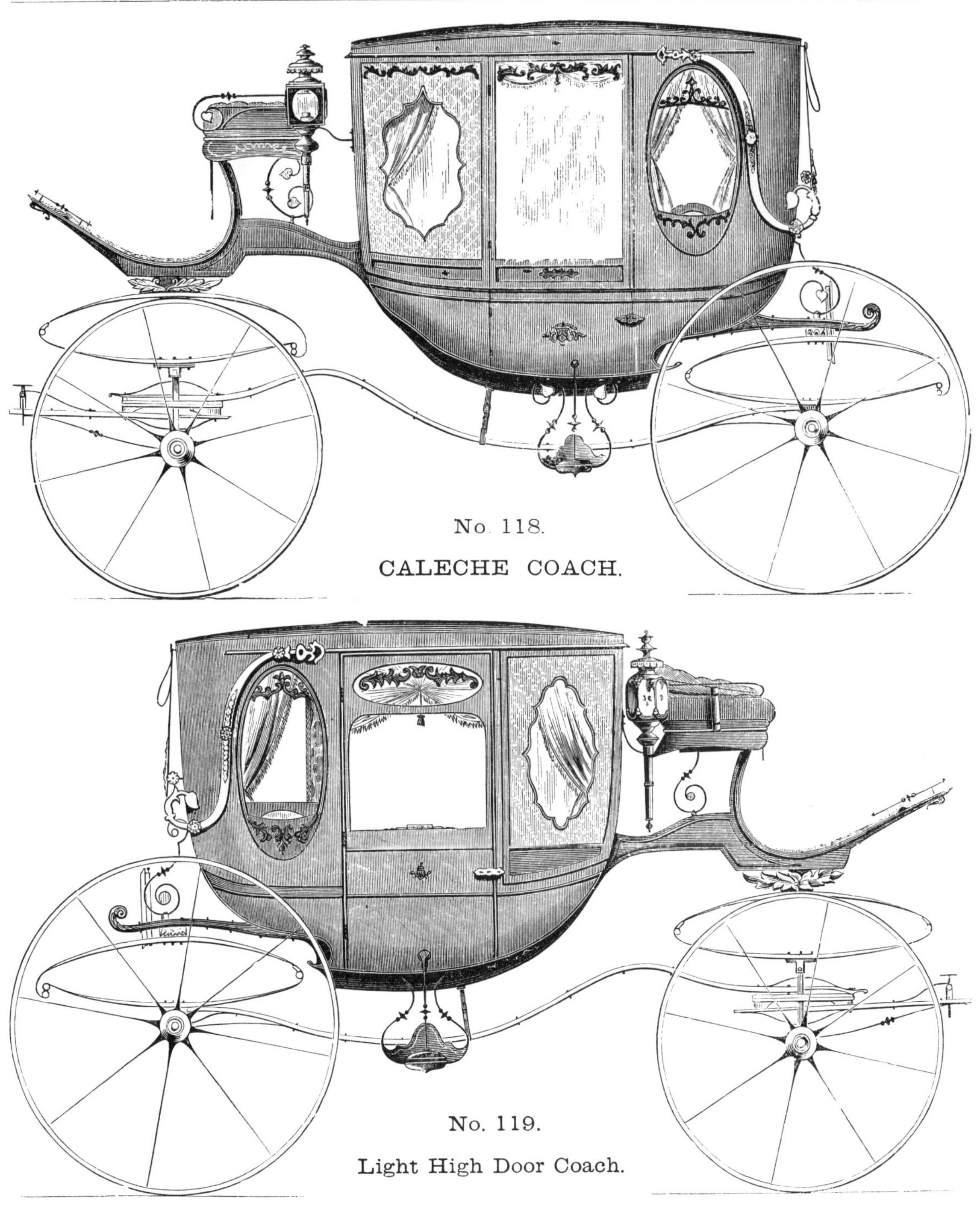

No. 118.

CALECHE COACH.

No. 119.

Light High Door Coach.

No. 120.—VERY LIGHT CALECHE COACH.

No. 121.—CHILD'S GIG.

No. 122.—Child's Phaeton.

No. 123.—C SPRING COACH.

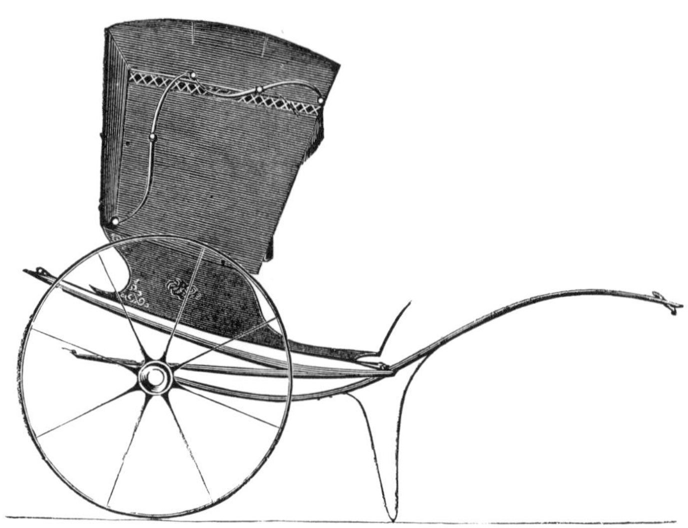

No. 124.—Child's Chaise.

No. 125.—Crane Neck Caleche Coach.

No. 126.—HIGH DOOR COACH.

No. 127.—Child's Chaise.

Lawrence, Bradley & Pardee,

HARNESS.

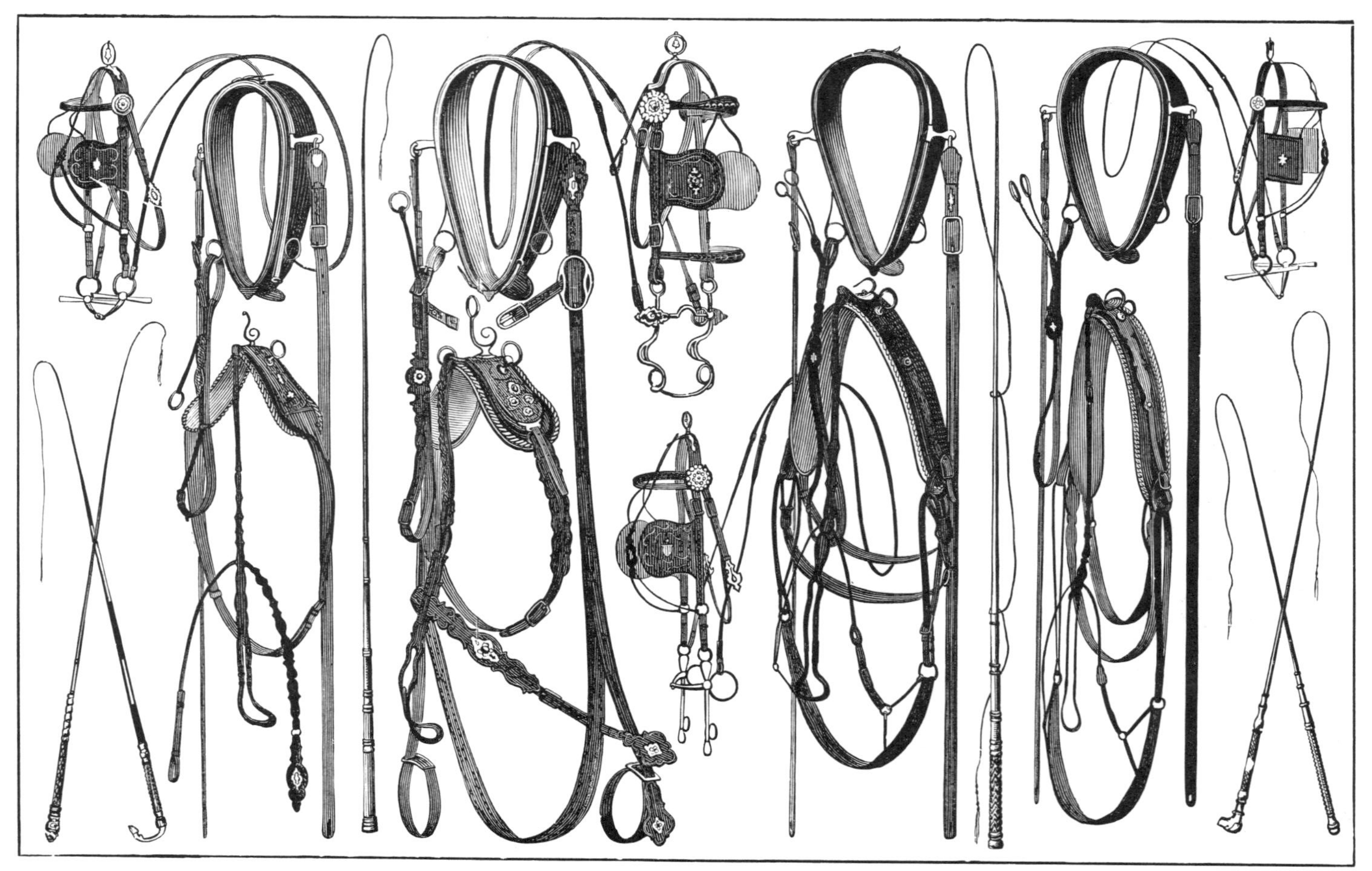

No. 1.—Light Shifting. No. 2.—Heavy Coach. No. 3.—Fine Single. No. 4.—Plain Single.

New Haven, Conn.

TONTINE HOTEL.

Fronting the New Haven Green, corner of Church and Court Sts.

H. L. SCRANTON, PROPRIETOR.

No. 128.—CHARIOT

No. 129.—CLARENCE.

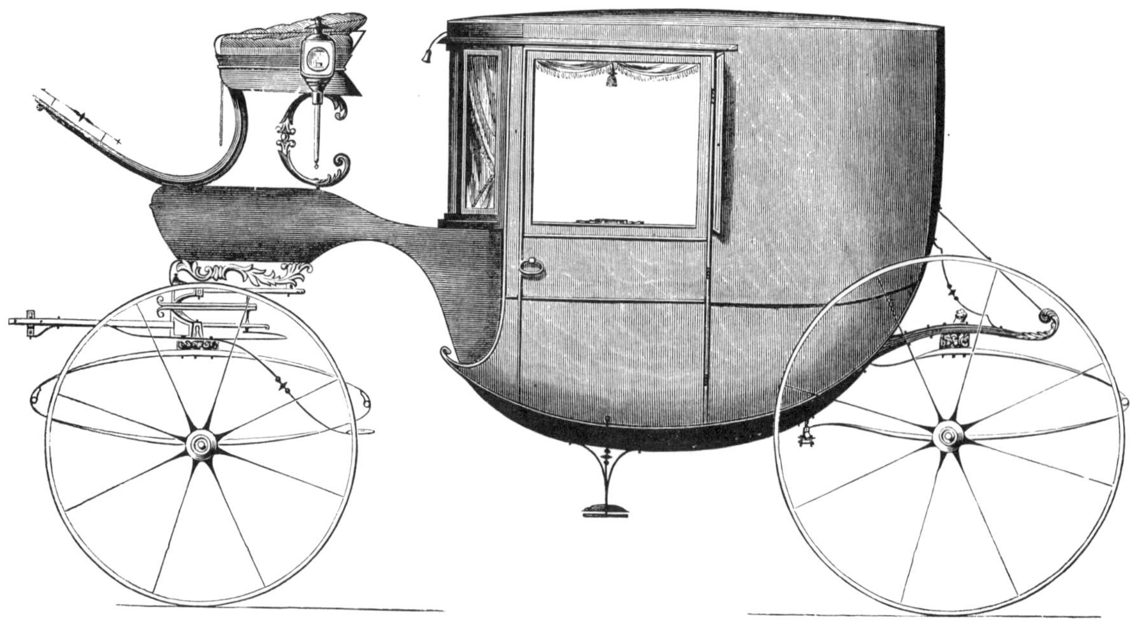

No. 130.—FRENCH CLARENCE.

No. 131.—COUPE.

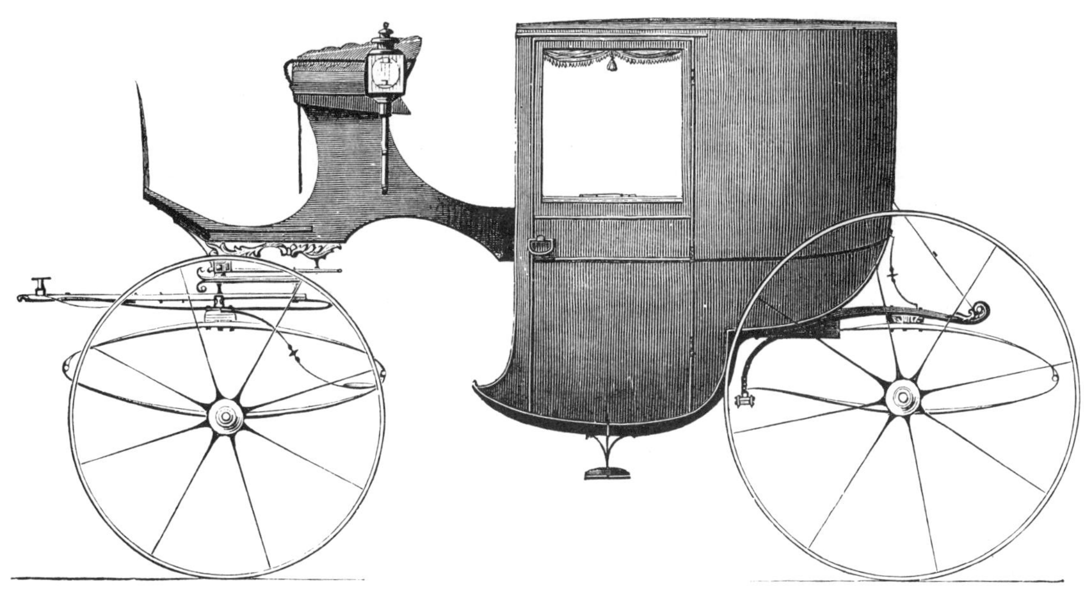

No. 132.—COUPE.

No. 133.—FRENCH COUPE.

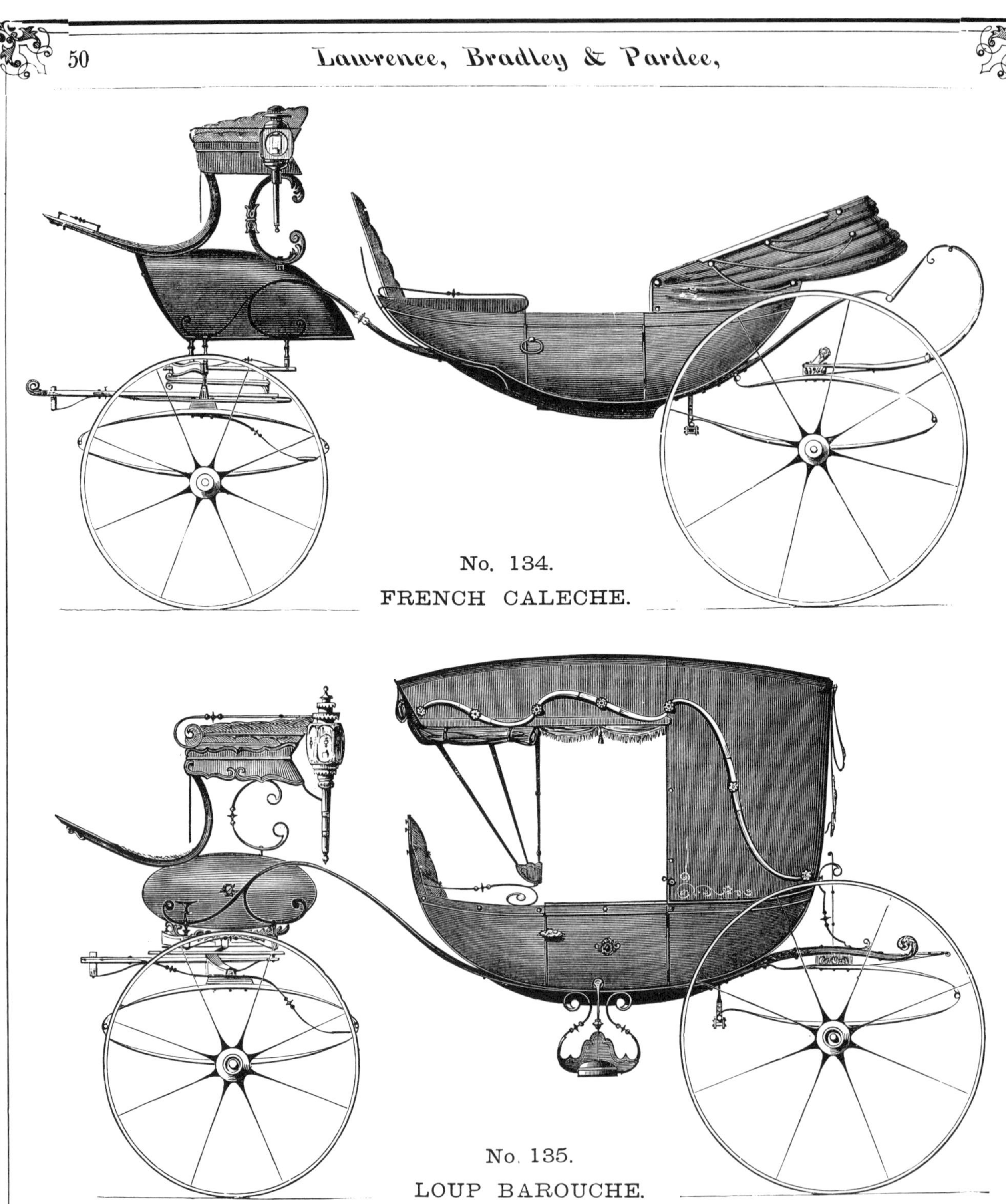

No. 134.
FRENCH CALECHE.

No. 135.
LOUP BAROUCHE.

No. 136.—Sociable Half-Top Caleche.

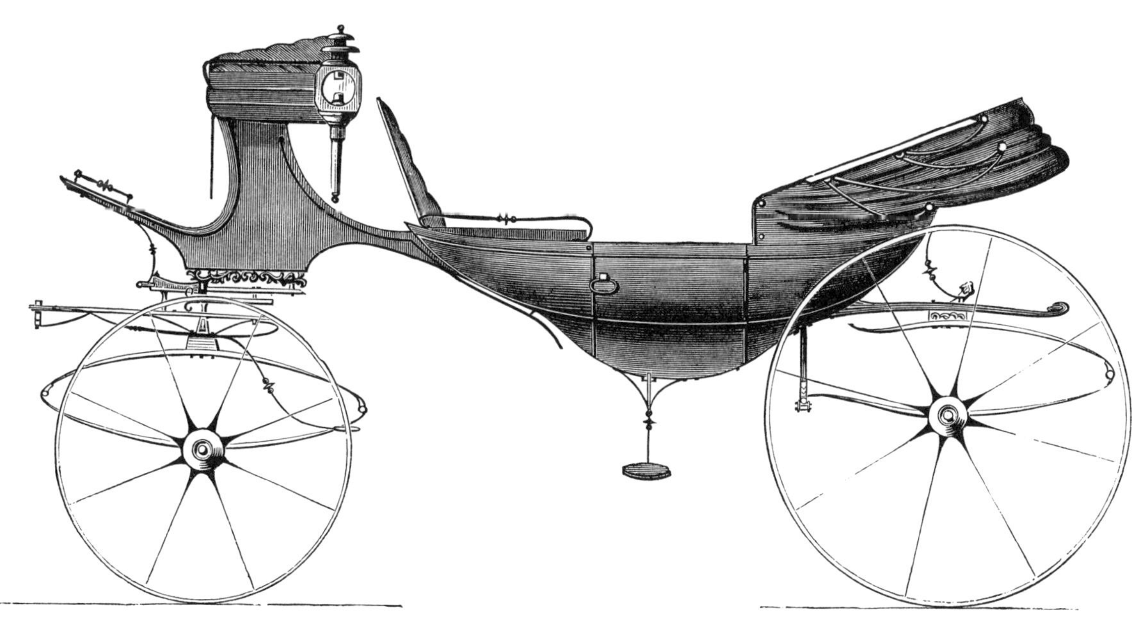

No. 137.—Sociable Half-Top Caleche.

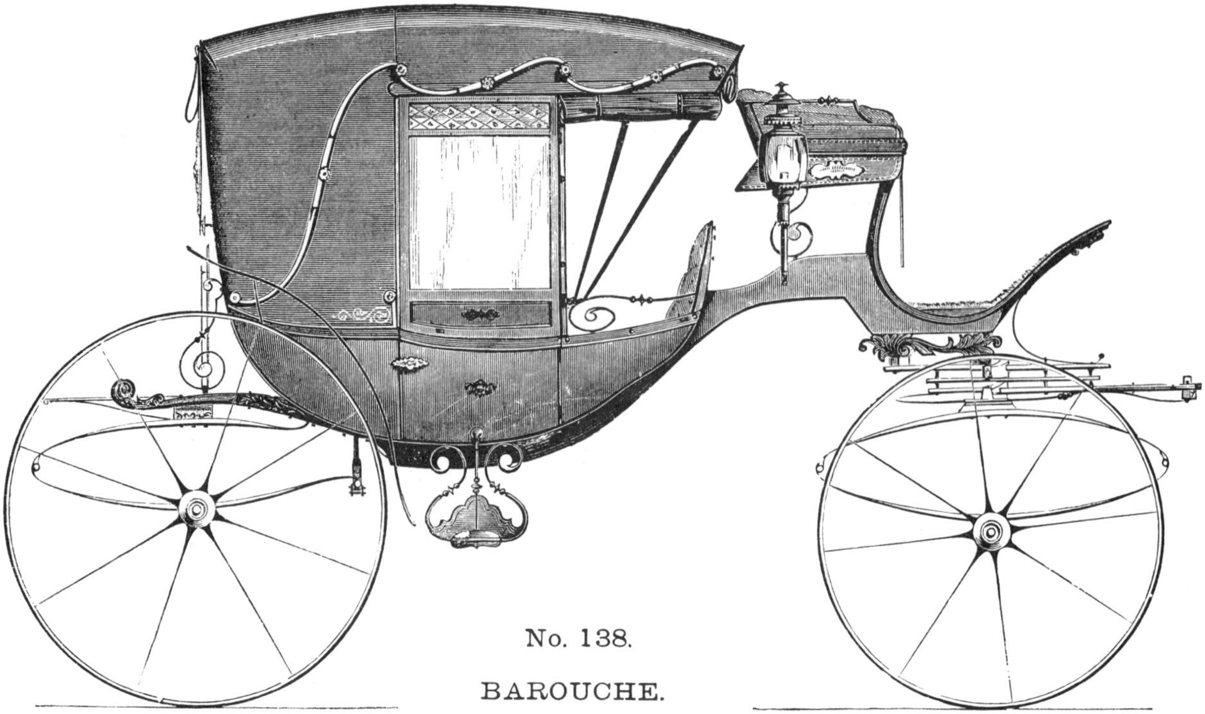

No. 138.

BAROUCHE.

No. 139.

GLADSTONE.

No. 140.—Crane Neck Brett.

No. 141.—CALECHE.

No. 142.—Light Crane Neck Barouche.

No. 143.—CALECHE.

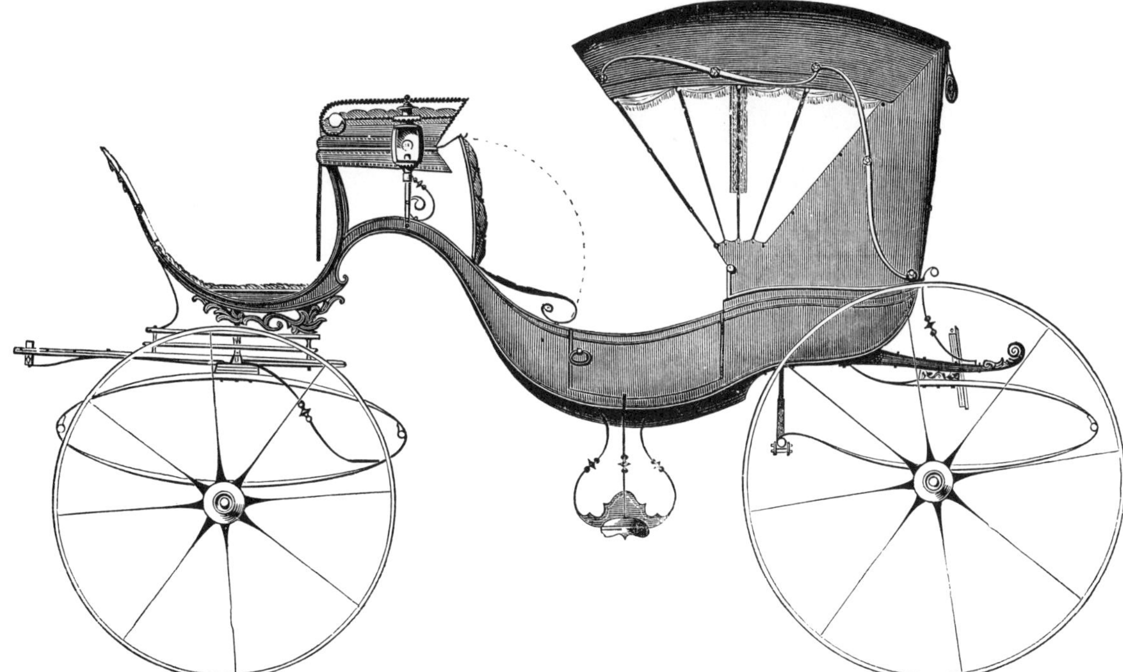

No. 144.—Crane Neck Brett.

No. 145.—Light Britzka.

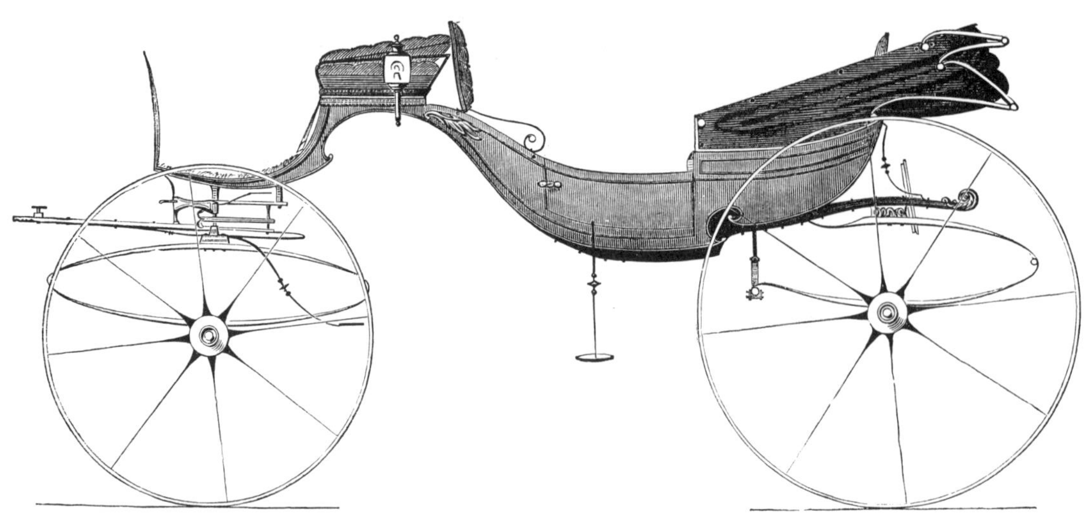

No. 146—Light Half-Top Barouche.

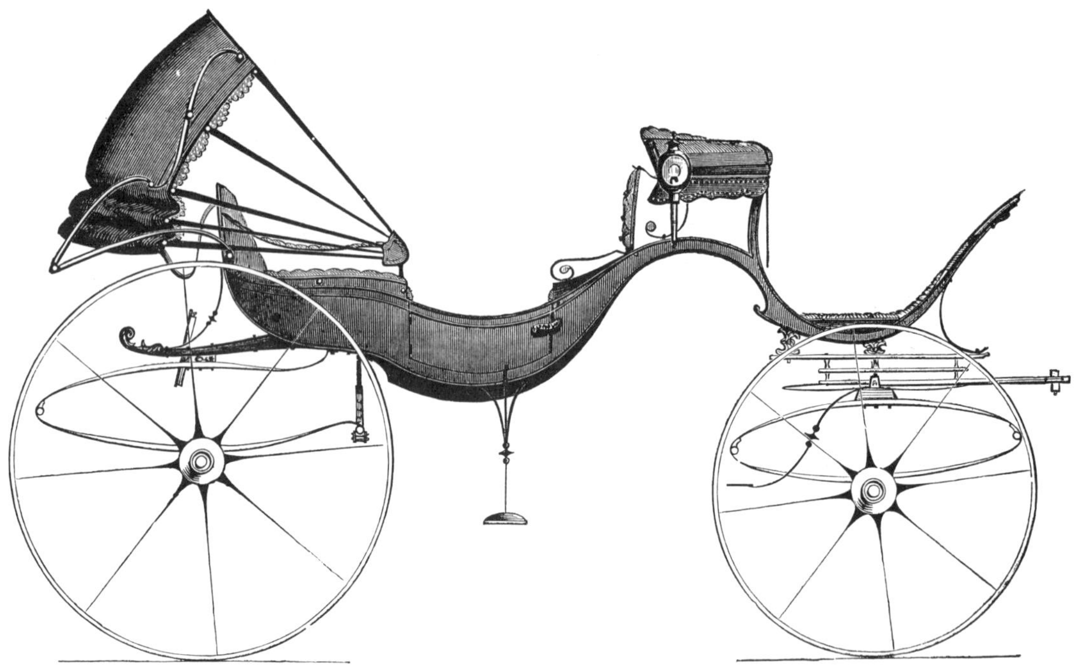

No. 147.—Crane Neck Brett.

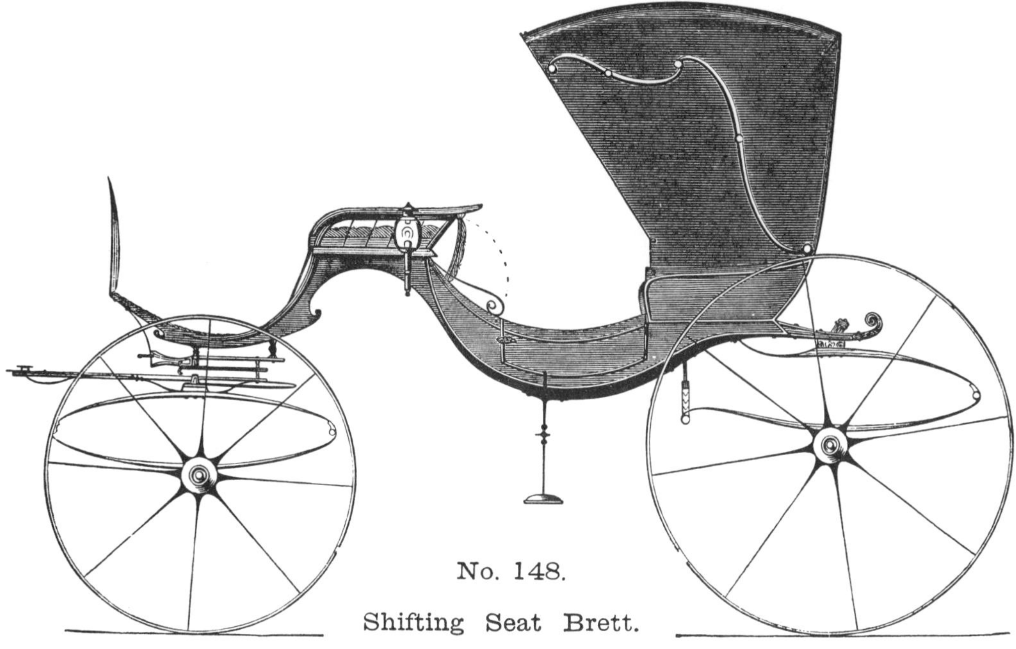

No. 148.

Shifting Seat Brett.

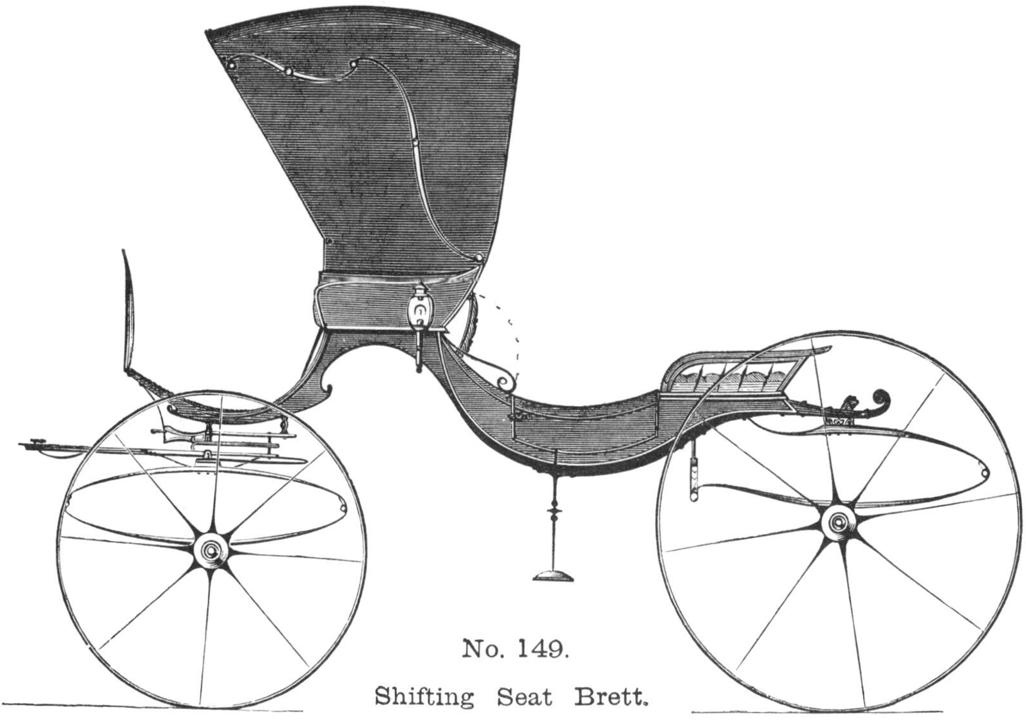

No. 149.

Shifting Seat Brett.

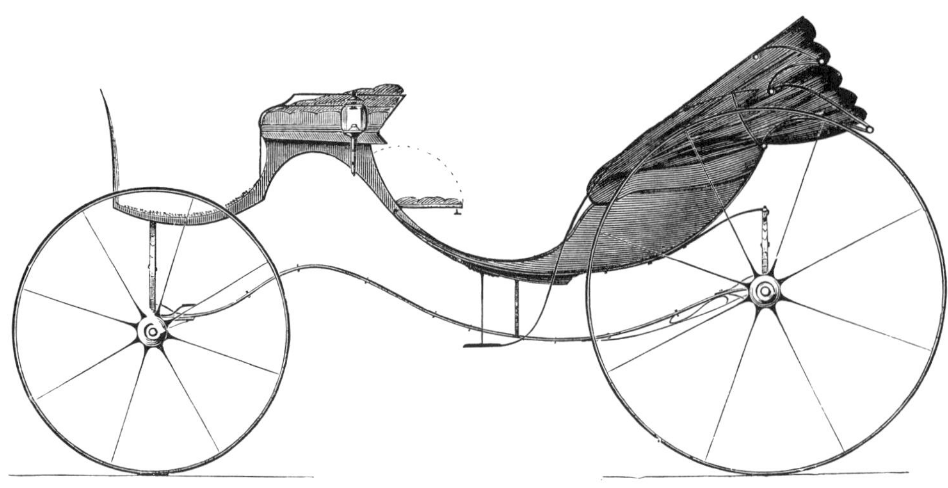

No. 150.— CABRIOLE.

No. 151.— Dickey Seat Brett.

No. 152.
Gipsy Brett.

No. 153.
CABRIOLE.

No. 154.—LOOP VICTORIA.

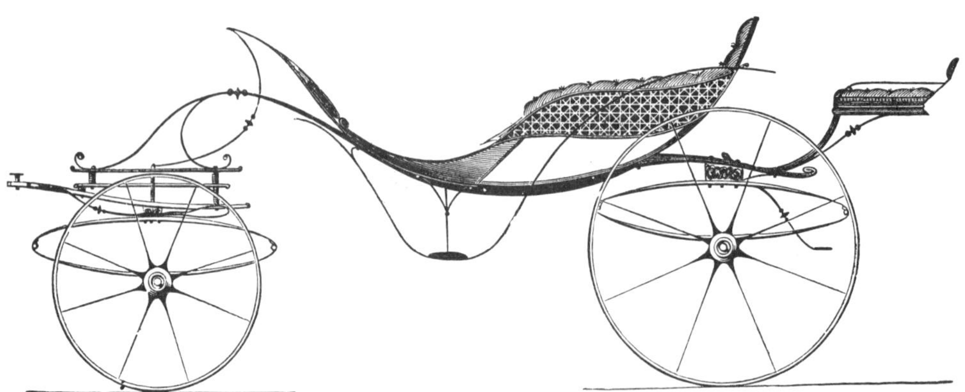

No. 155.—VICTORIA PHAETON.

No. 156.—LOOP VICTORIA.

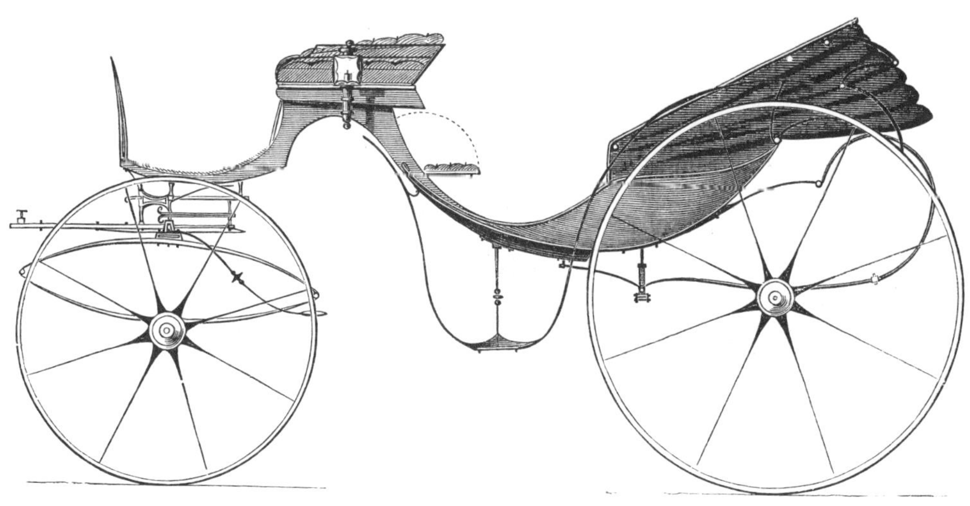

No. 157.—C SPRING VICTORIA.

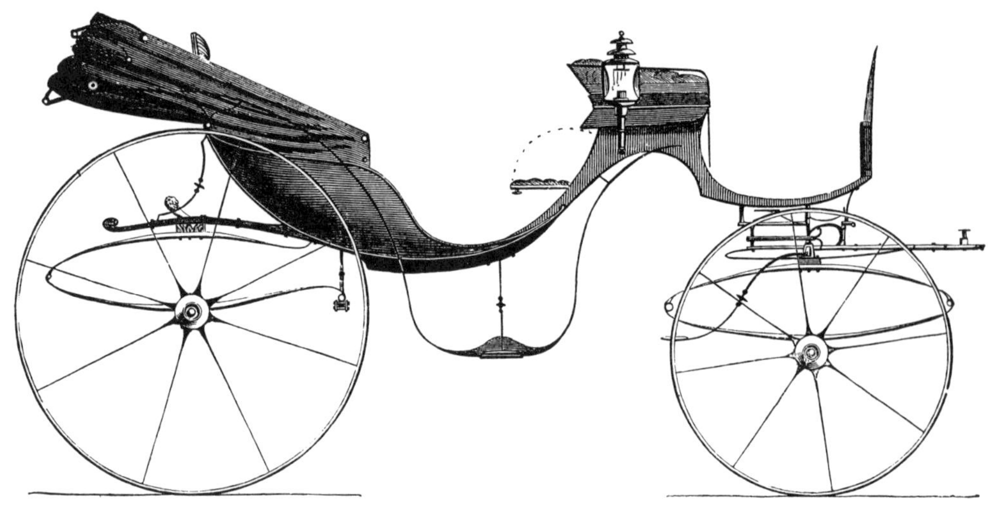

No. 158.— VICTORIA.

No. 159.— VICTORIA.

No. 160.—VICTORIA.

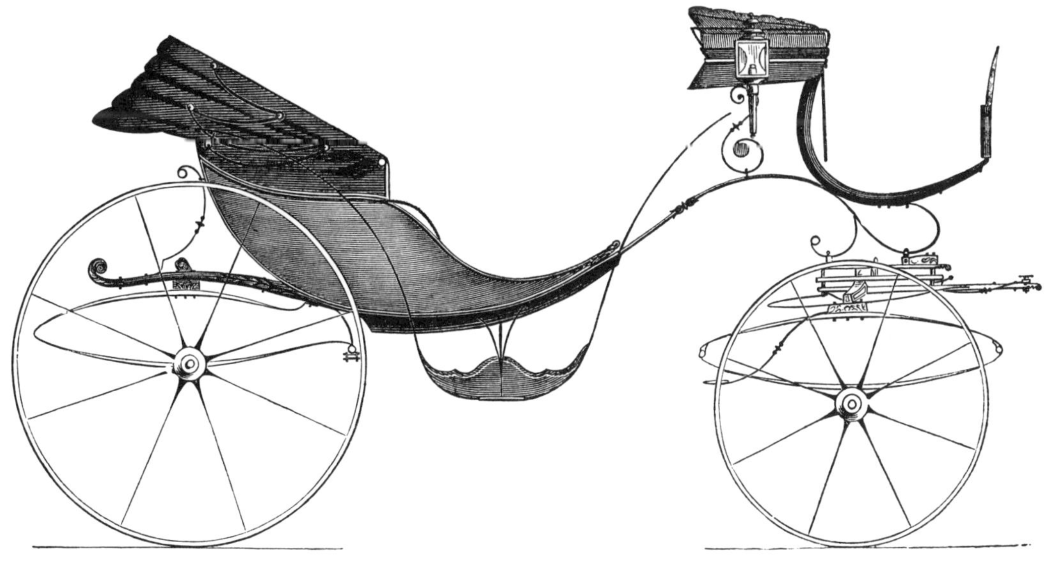

No. 161.—VICTORIA.

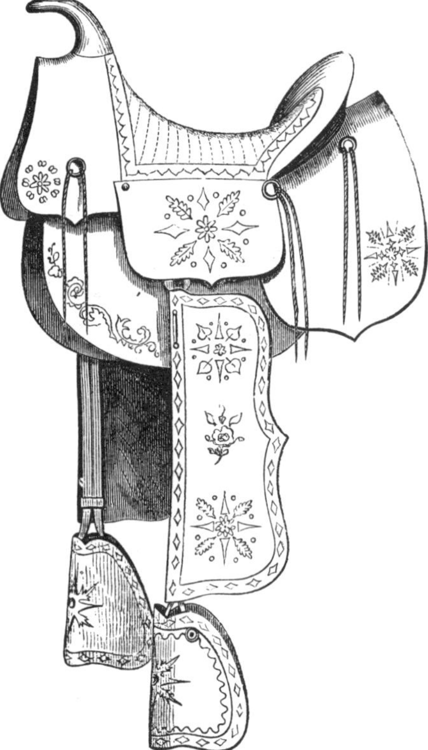

No. 1.—San Antonio.

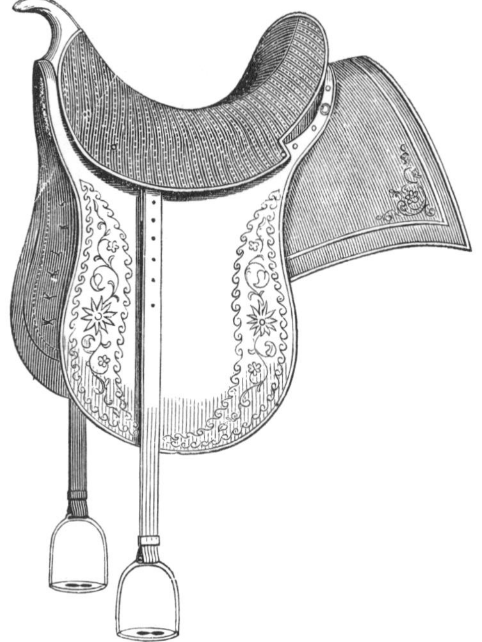

No. 2.—Spanish Horn.

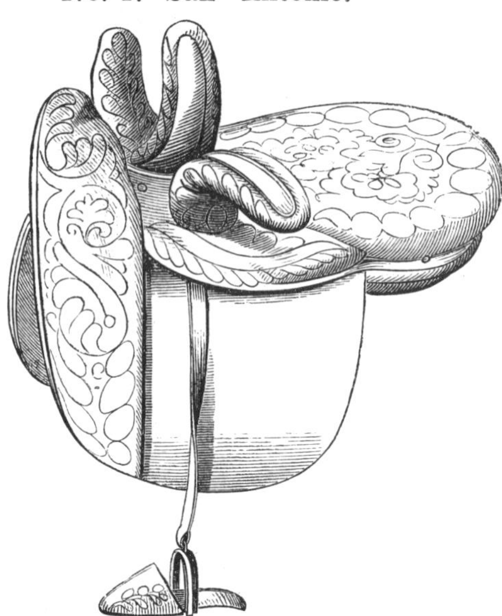

No. 4.—Fine Leaping Horn Side.

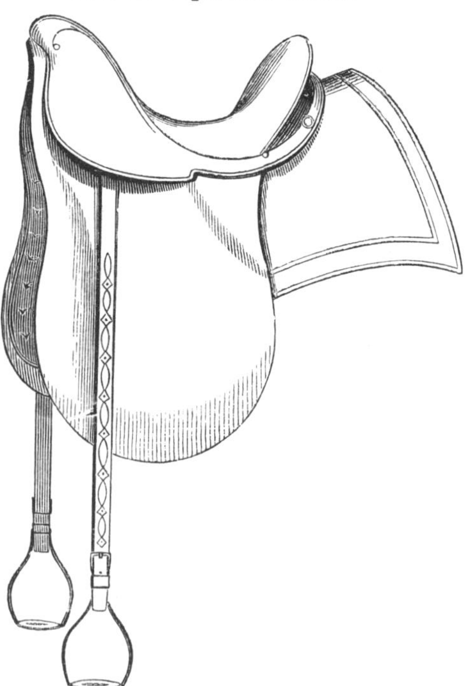

No. 3.—Smith.

FLORA TEMPLE, the "Queen of the Turf."

Owned by Wm. Macdonald, Esq., Baltimore.

FLORA TEMPLE is a light bay mare, 14 hands $1\frac{1}{4}$ inch high, and weighs in trotting condition, 835 pounds. She was foaled in 1846, in Sangerfield, Oneida Co., N. Y. out of Madam Temple, by One-Eyed Hunter; he by the well-known Kentucky Hunter. She made her first appearance in public on the Red House track in 1850, beating the White Pony in a single mile dash; and in the same year, on the Union Course, L. I., under the name of Flora, won a race, mile heats in harness, beating Whitehall and three others. Flora has been entered in ninty-five races, winning seventy-five, receiving forfeit in five, and two drawn—and has beaten all the more celebrated horses known to the American turf. In her renowned match with Princess, at Kalamazoo, Michigan, in 1859, she made the wonderful time of 2:19$\frac{3}{4}$, which is unequaled in the Turf records of the world, and establishing, beyond question, her right to the title of "Queen of the Turf."

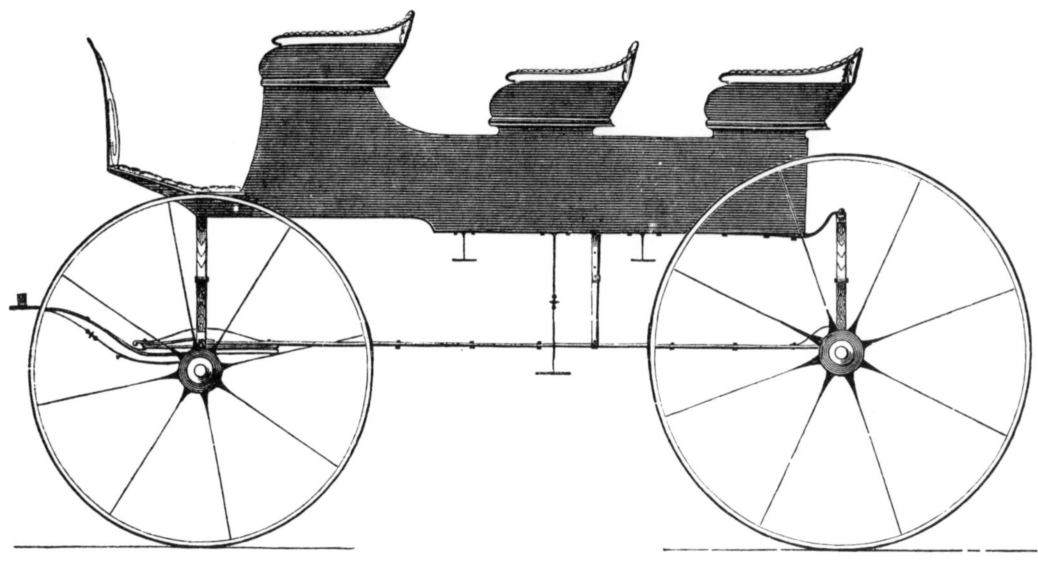

No. 162.—Six Seat Beach Wagon.

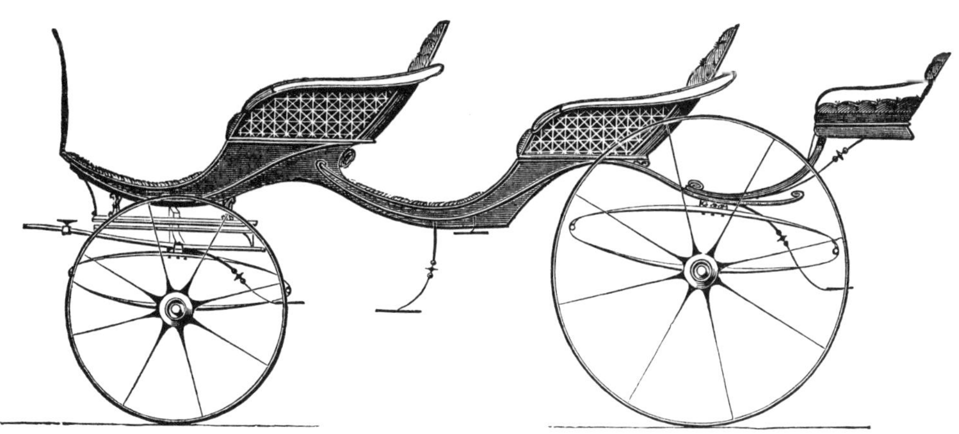

No. 163.—Siamese Phaeton.

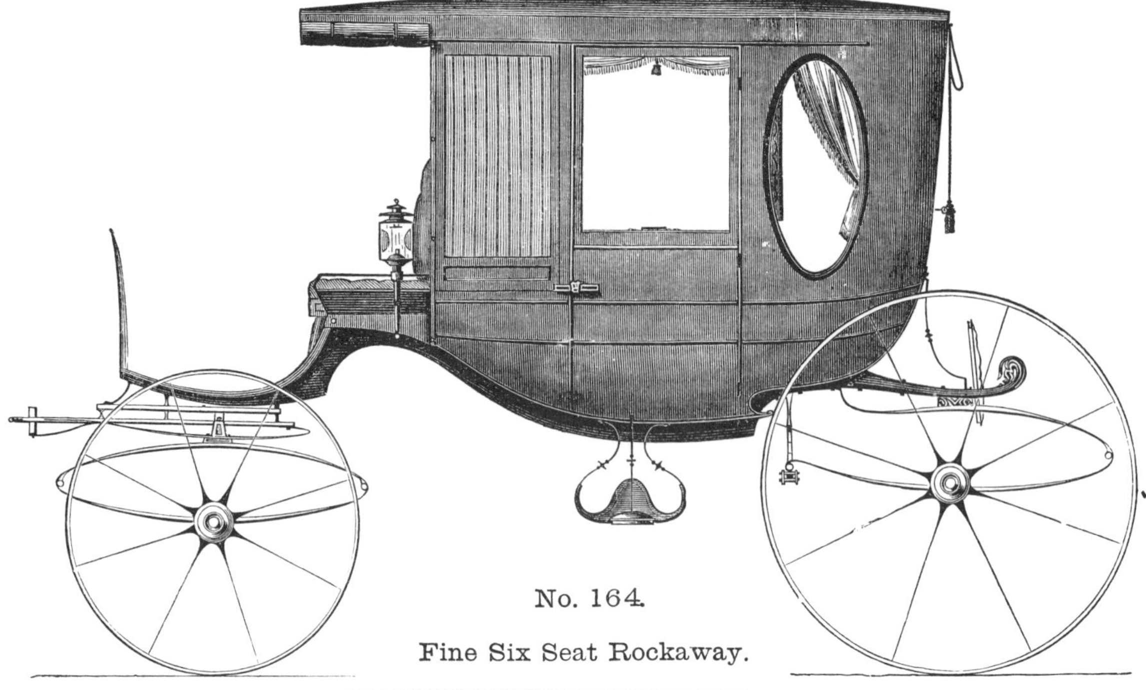

No. 164.

Fine Six Seat Rockaway.

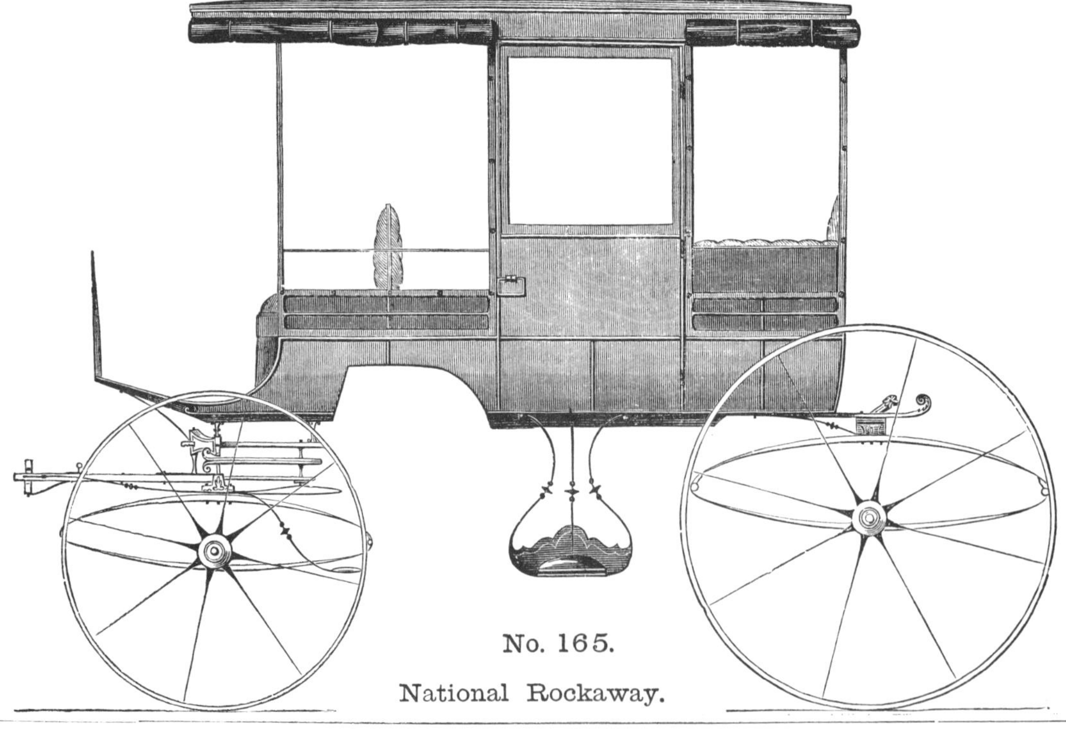

No. 165.

National Rockaway.

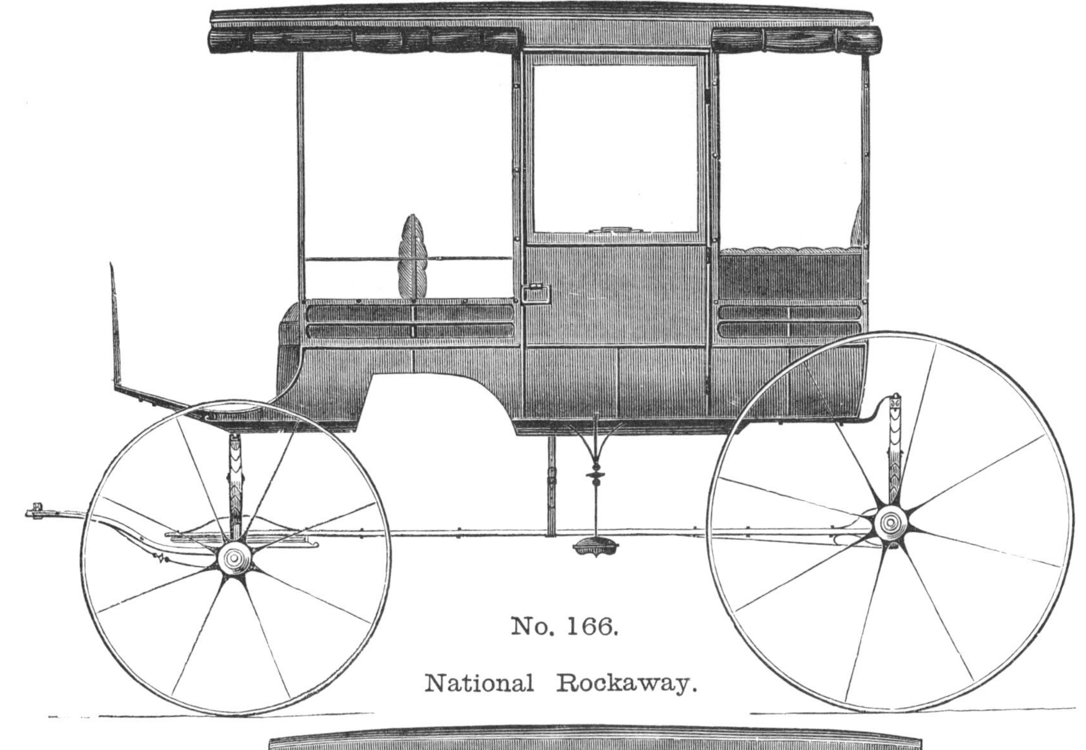

No. 166.

National Rockaway.

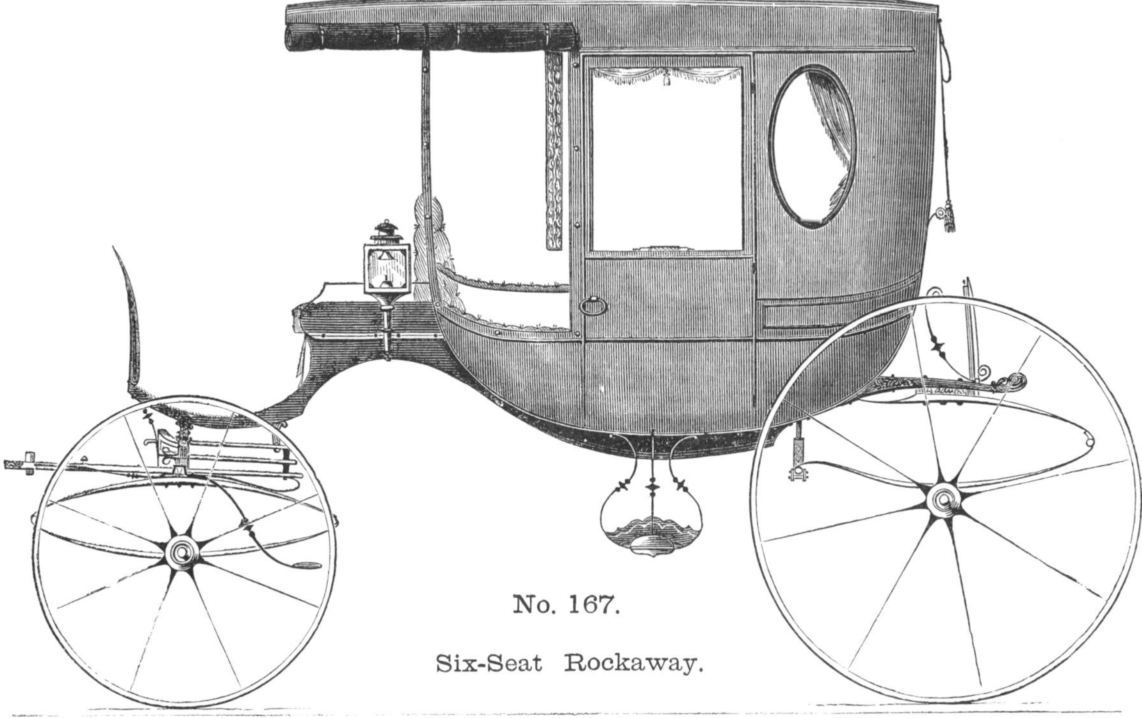

No. 167.

Six-Seat Rockaway.

No. 168.

Six Seat Rockaway.

No. 169.

Curtain Rockaway.

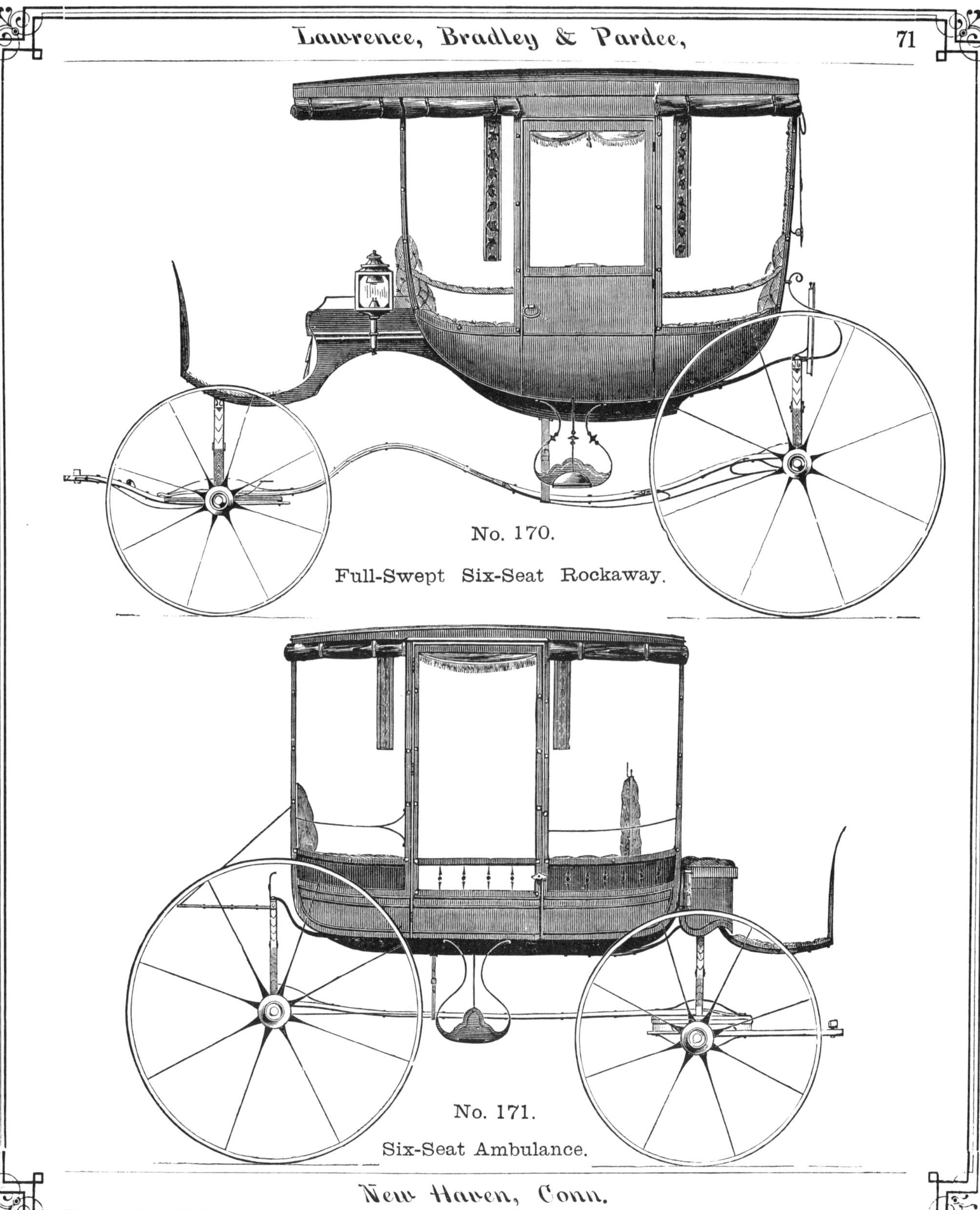

No. 170.

Full-Swept Six-Seat Rockaway.

No. 171.

Six-Seat Ambulance.

No. 172.

Light, Open, Five-Seat Rockaway.

No. 173.

Skeleton Six-Seat Rockaway.

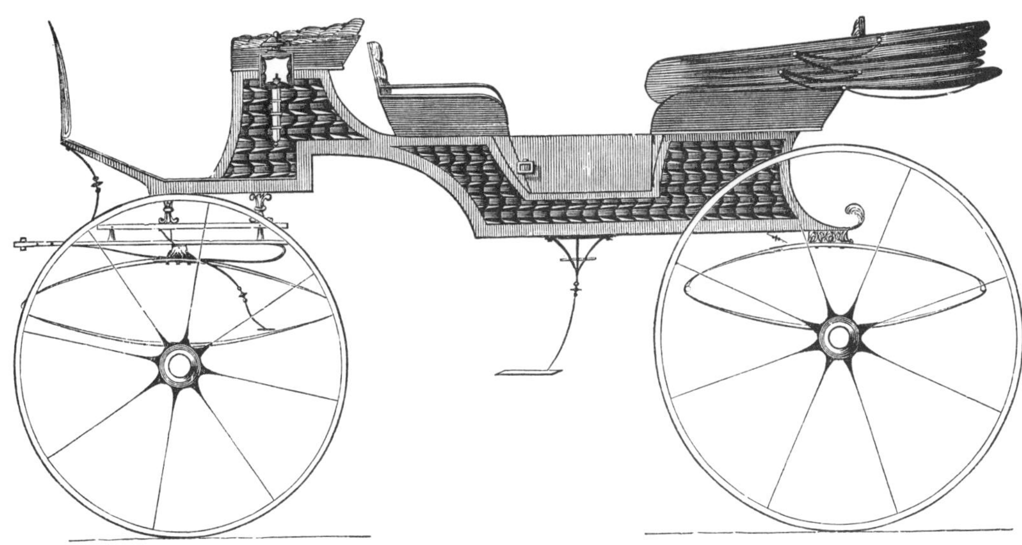

No. 174.—American Six-Seat Phaeton.

No. 175.—German Six-Seat Phaeton.

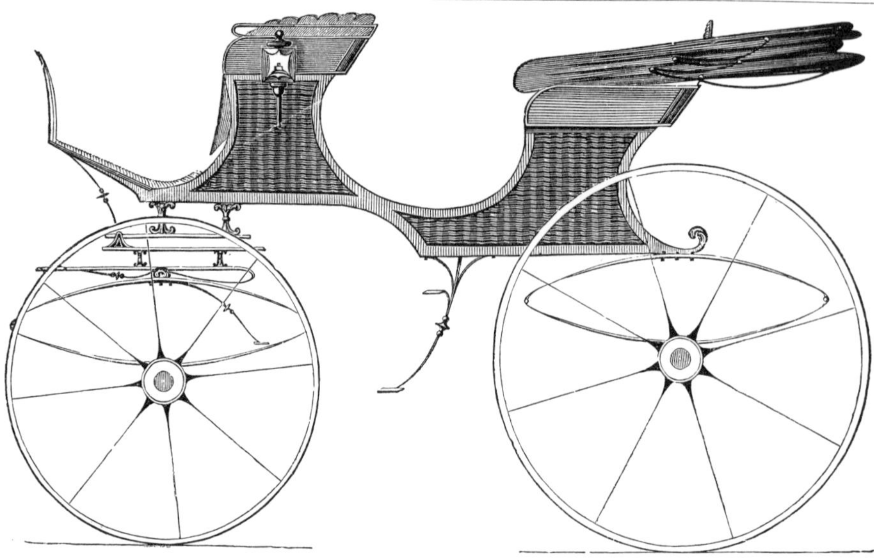

No. 176.—Central Park Phaeton.

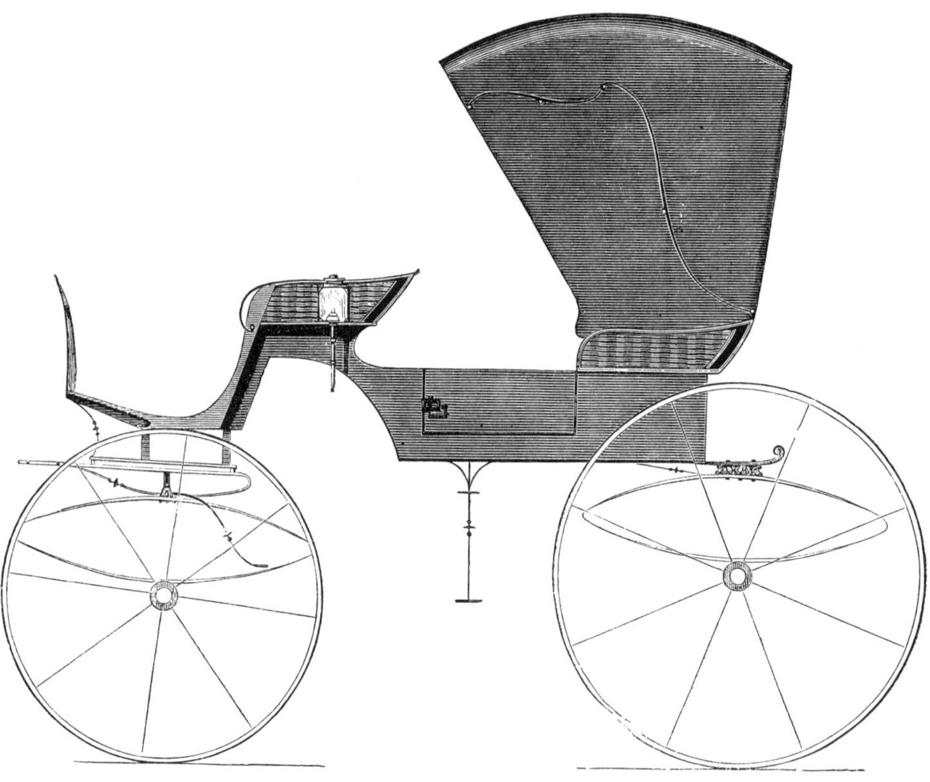

No. 177.—American Phaeton.

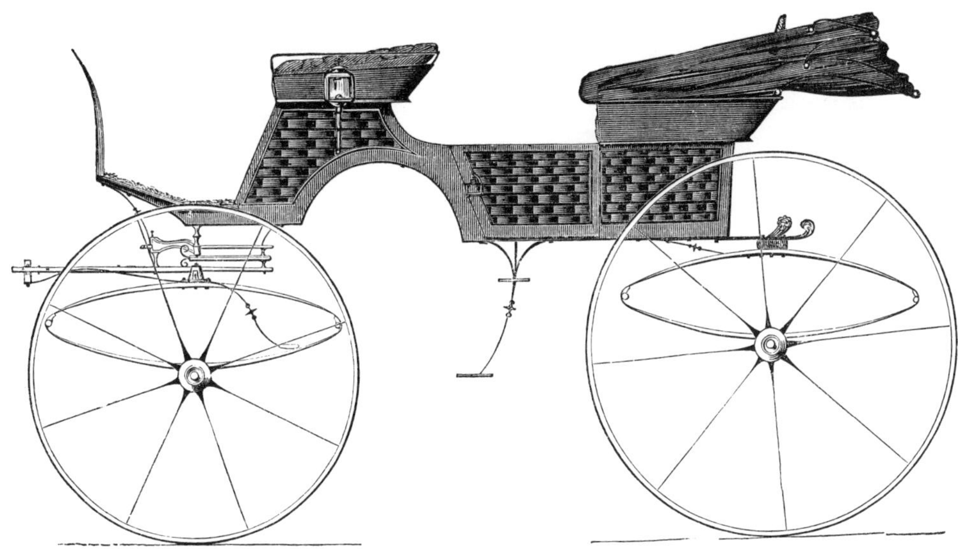

No. 178.—French Phaeton.

No. 179.—King Phaeton.

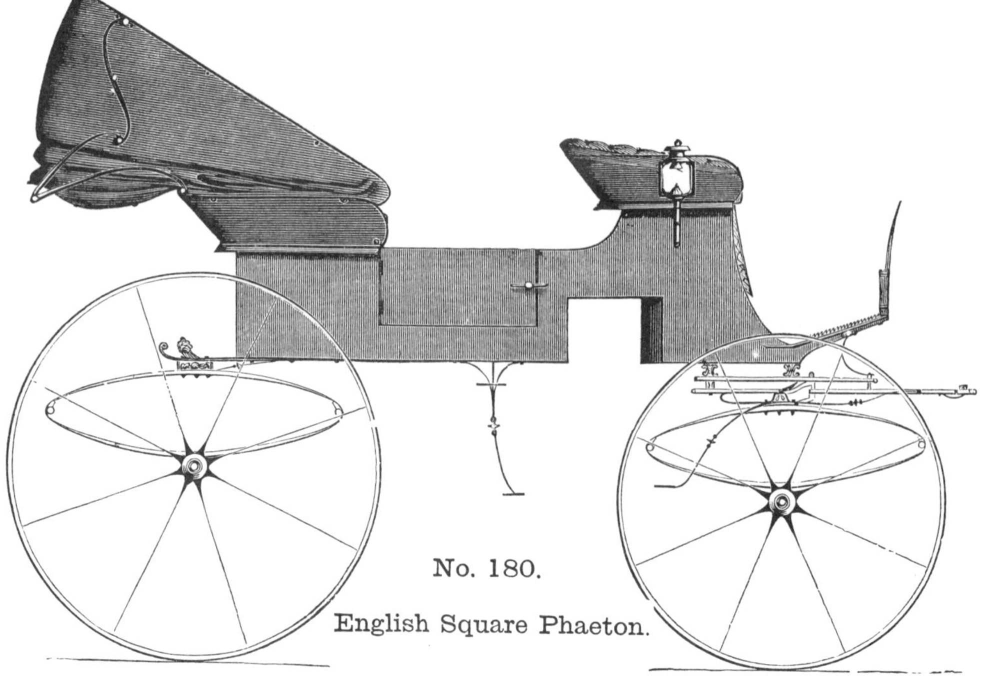

No. 180.
English Square Phaeton.

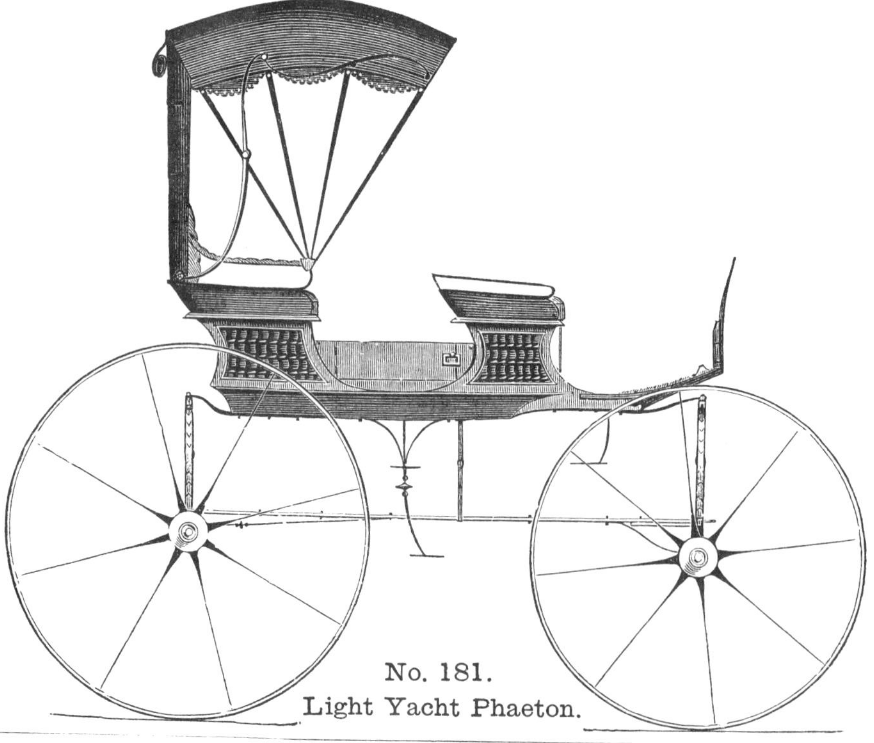

No. 181.
Light Yacht Phaeton.

No. 182.—Shifting Seat Box Wagon.

No. 183.—Shifting Seat Phaeton.

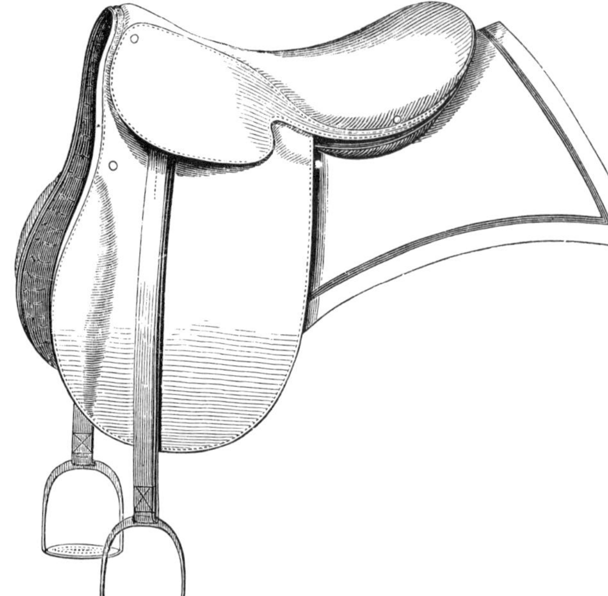

No. 5.—English, with Cloth.

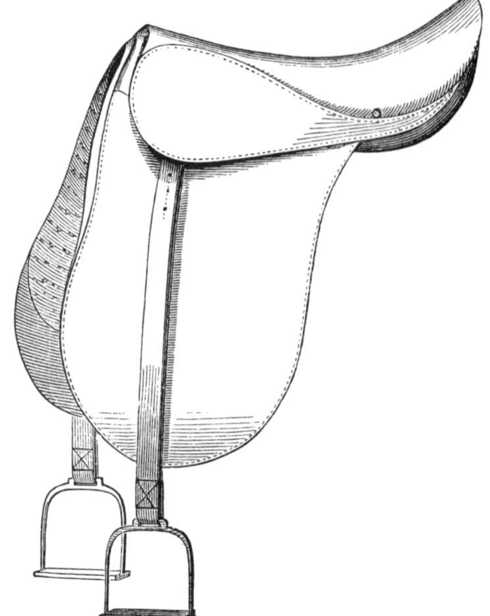

No. 6.—Straight Head.

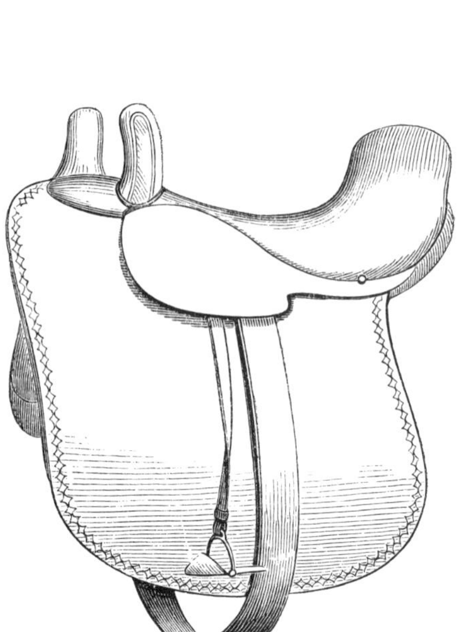

No. 7.—Common Side.

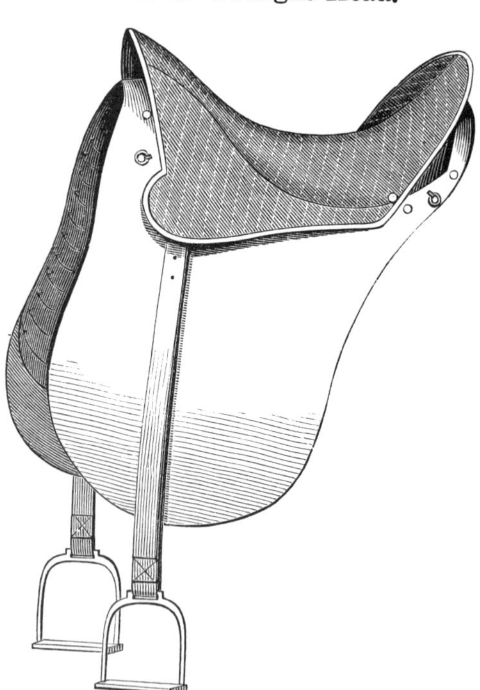

No. 8.—Spanish No-horn.

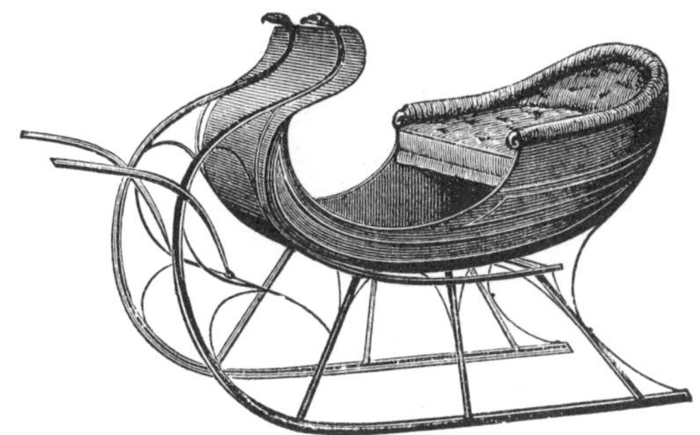

No. 184.—Albany Cutter.

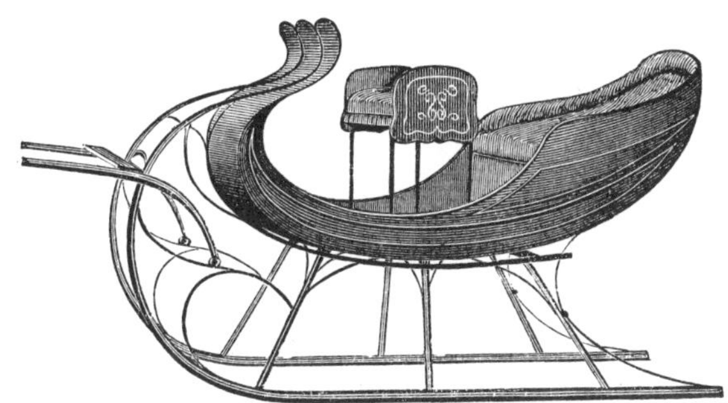

No. 185.—Light Two Seat Sleigh.

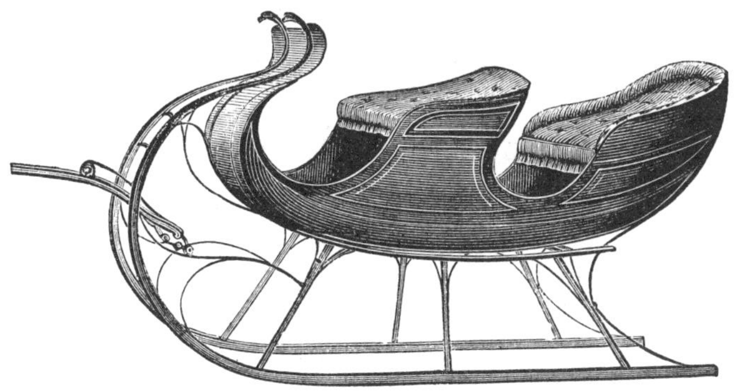

No. 186.—Fine Pony Sleigh.

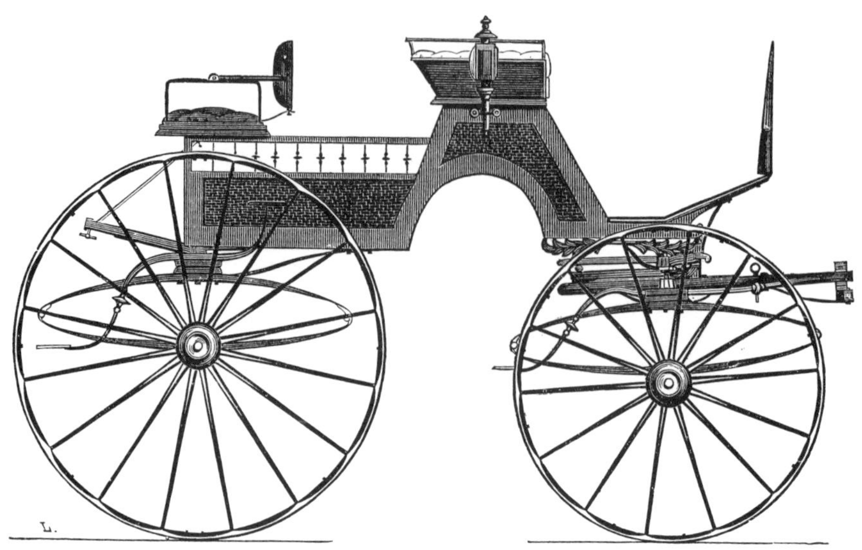

No. 187.—French Dog Cart.

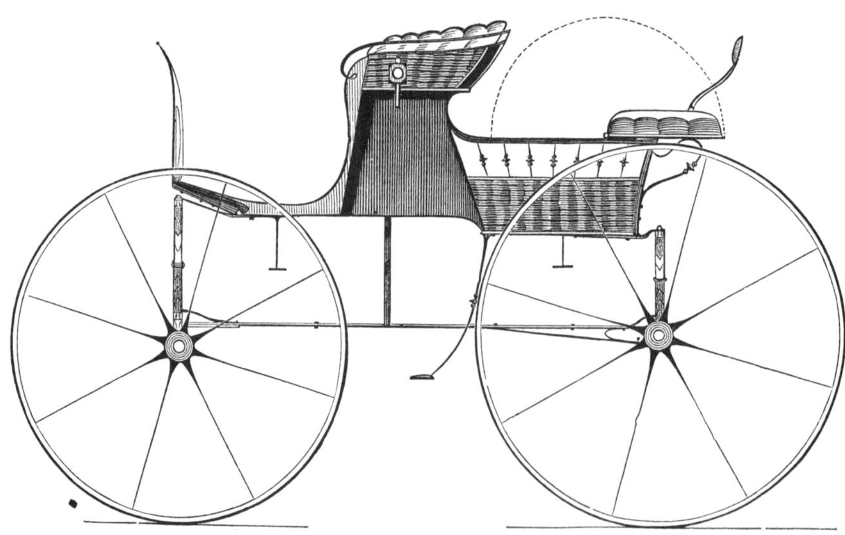

No. 188.—American Dog Cart.

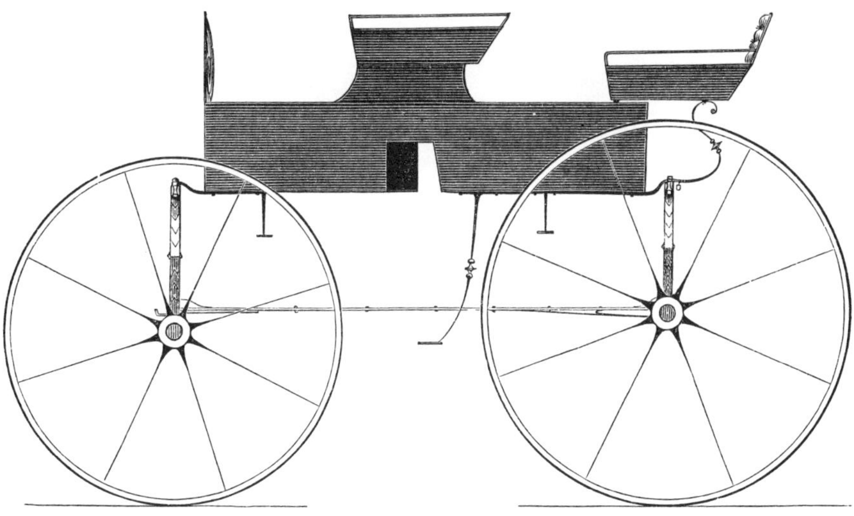

No. 189.—Shifting-Seat Box Wagon.

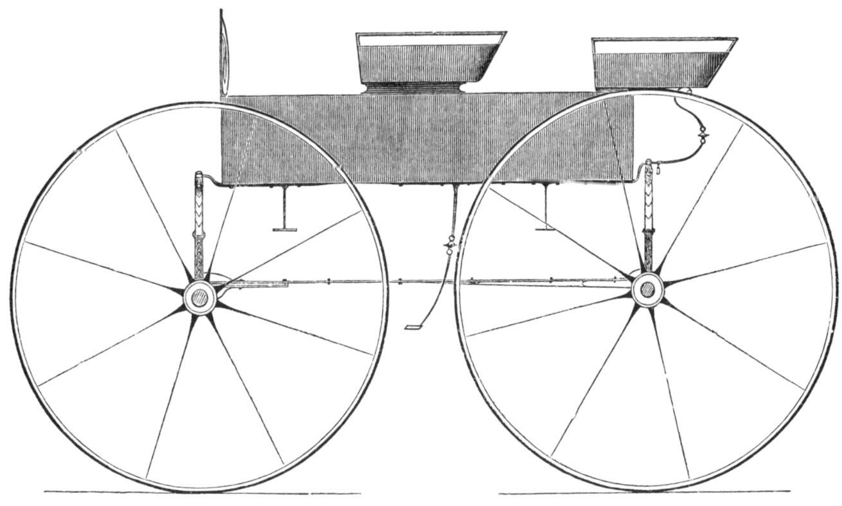

No. 190.—Light Box Wagon.

No. 191.—American Yacht Wagon.

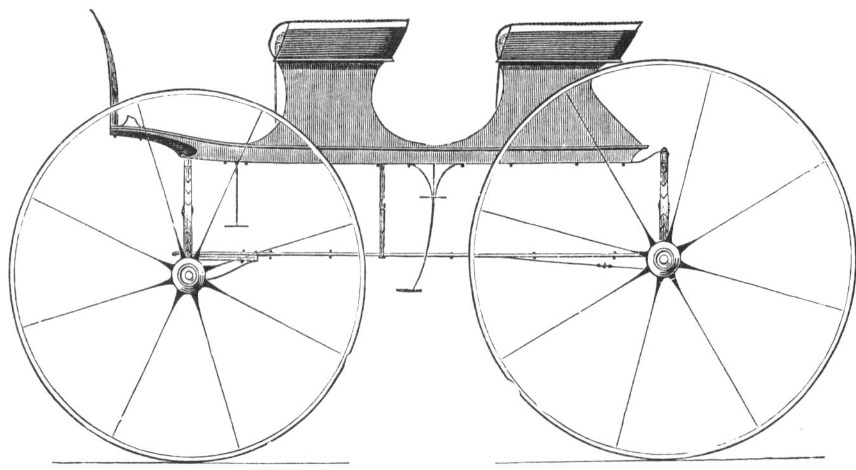

No. 192.—Clipper Wagon.

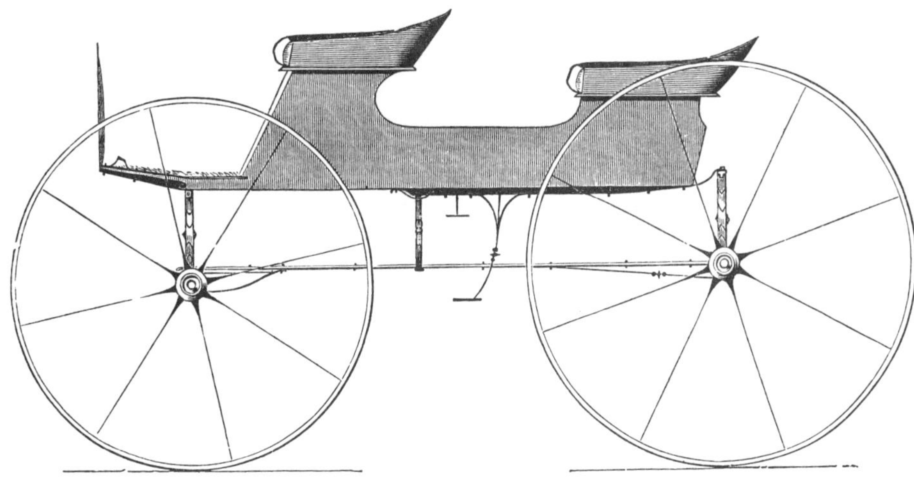

No. 193.—Popular Wagon.

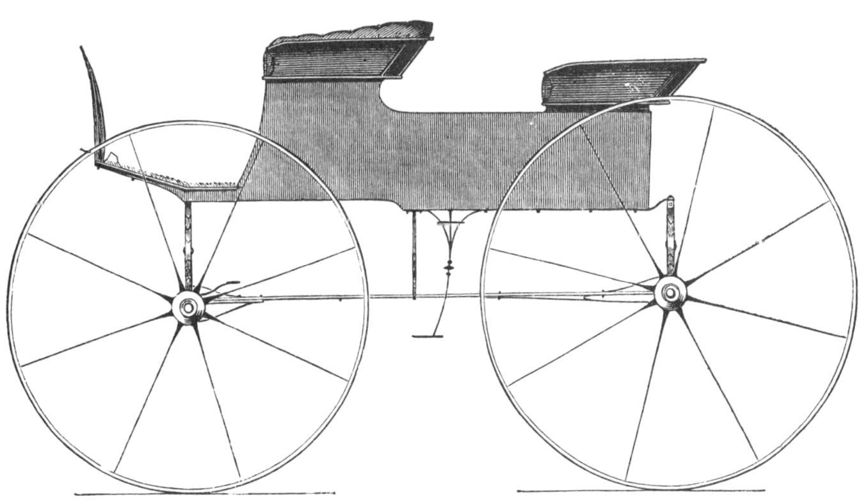

No. 194.—York Wagon.

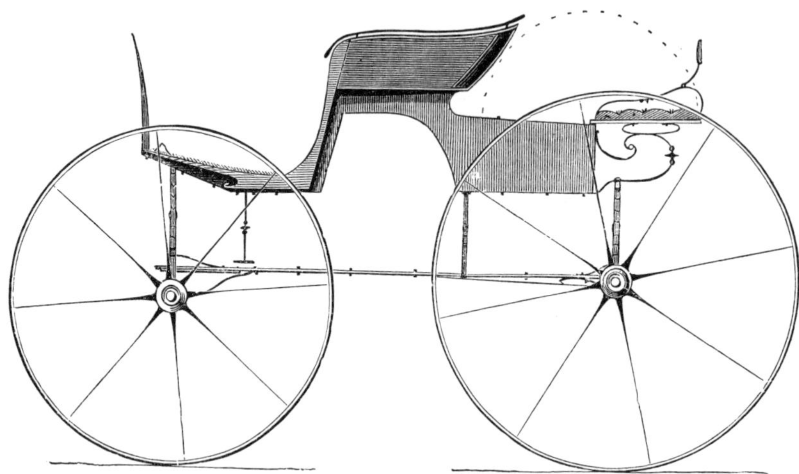

No. 195.—Cut-under Turn-Out-Seat Buggie.

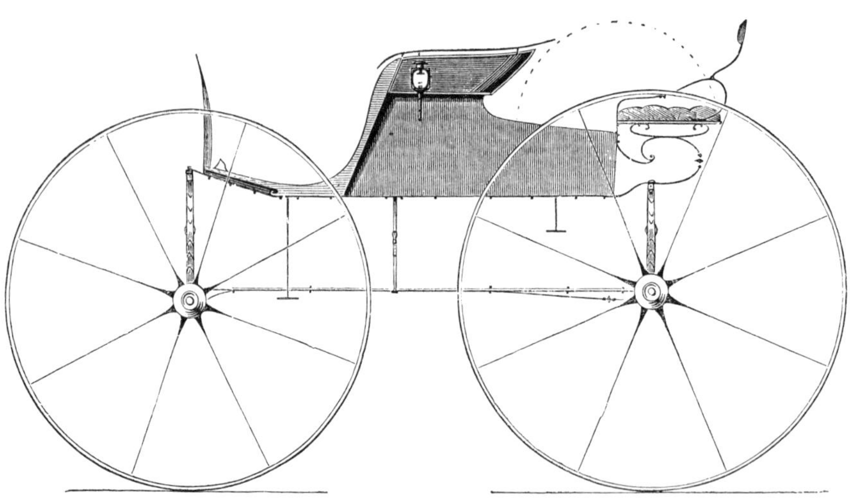

No. 196.—Sensible Buggie, with Turn-Out Seat.

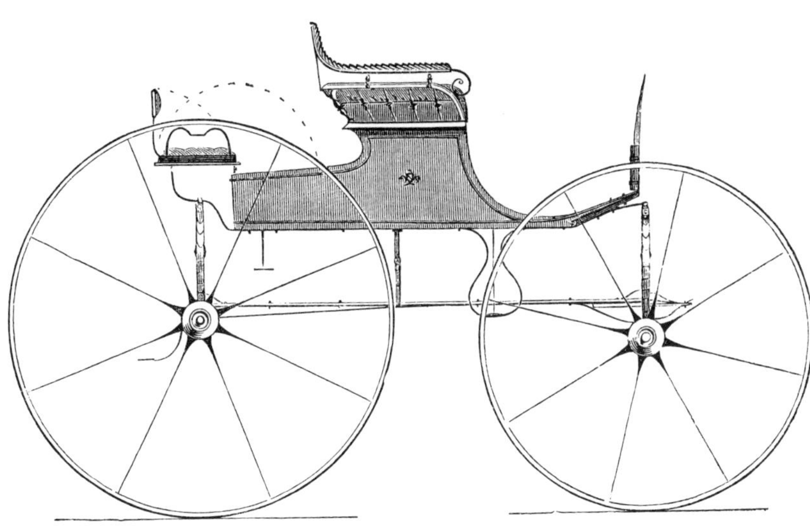

No. 197.—Turn-Out Seat Buggie.

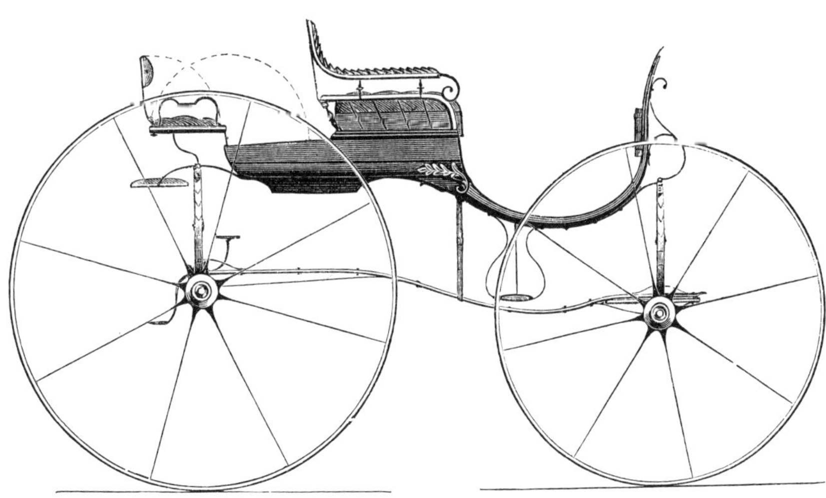

No. 198.—Drop-Front Buggie.

No. 199.—French Jump Seat.

No. 200.—Six-Seat Chariotee.

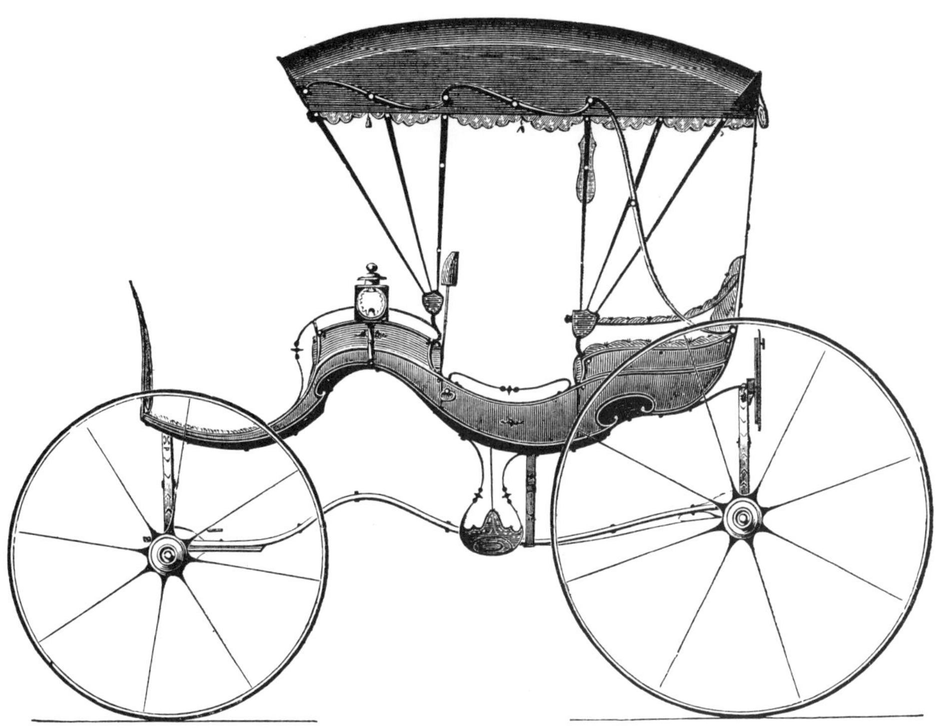

No. 201.—Unique Chariotee.

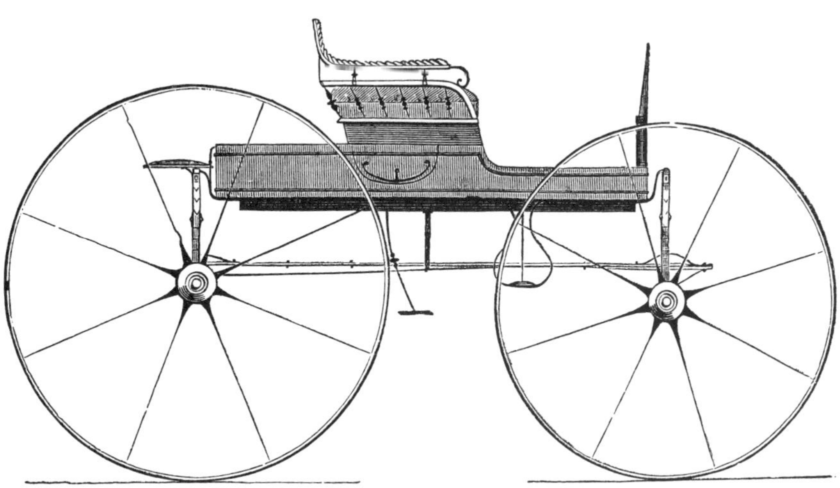

No. 202.—Slide-Seat No-Top.

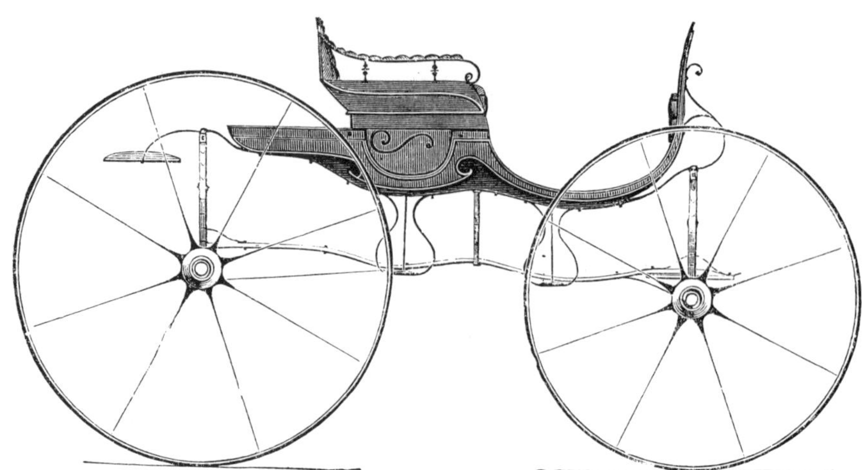

No. 203.—Slide-Seat No-Top.

No. 204.—Carved Chariotee.

No. 205.—English Chariotee.

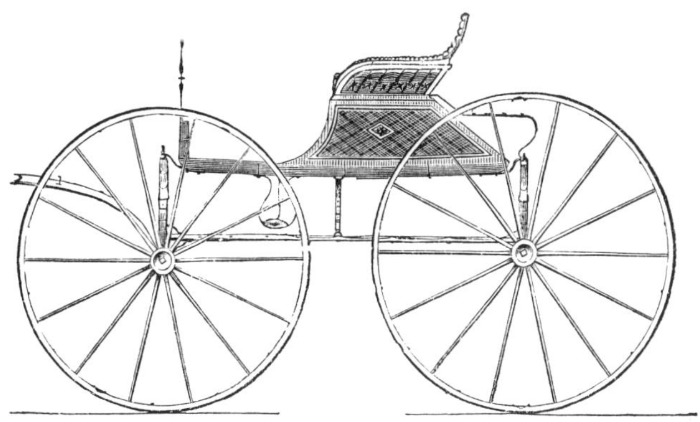

No. 206.—Wide-World No-Top Buggie.

No. 207.—Cut-Under No-Top Buggie.

No. 208.—Crane-Neck Chariotee.

No. 209.—Cabriolet Chariotee.

No. 210.—Plantation No-Top Buggie.

No. 211.—Antique No-Top Buggie.

No. 212.—French Chariotee.

No. 213.—American Yacht Shifting-Top Chariotee.

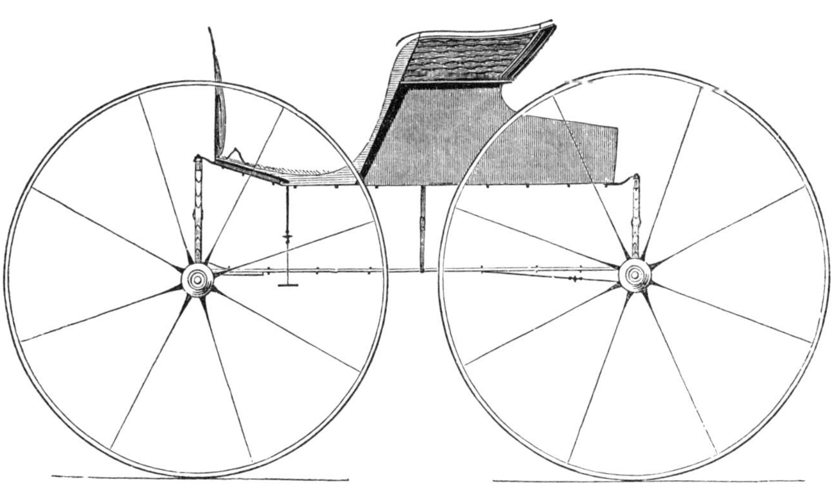

No. 214.—Sensible No-Top Buggie.

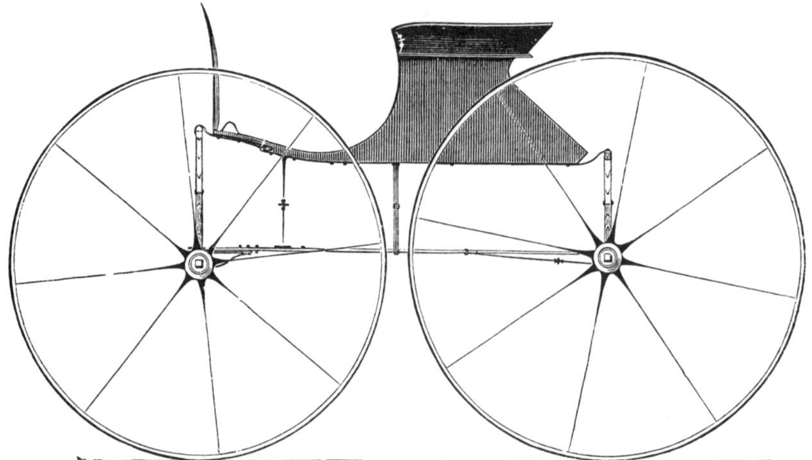

No. 215.—Excelsior Trotter.

No. 216.—Light Cabriolet Chariotee.

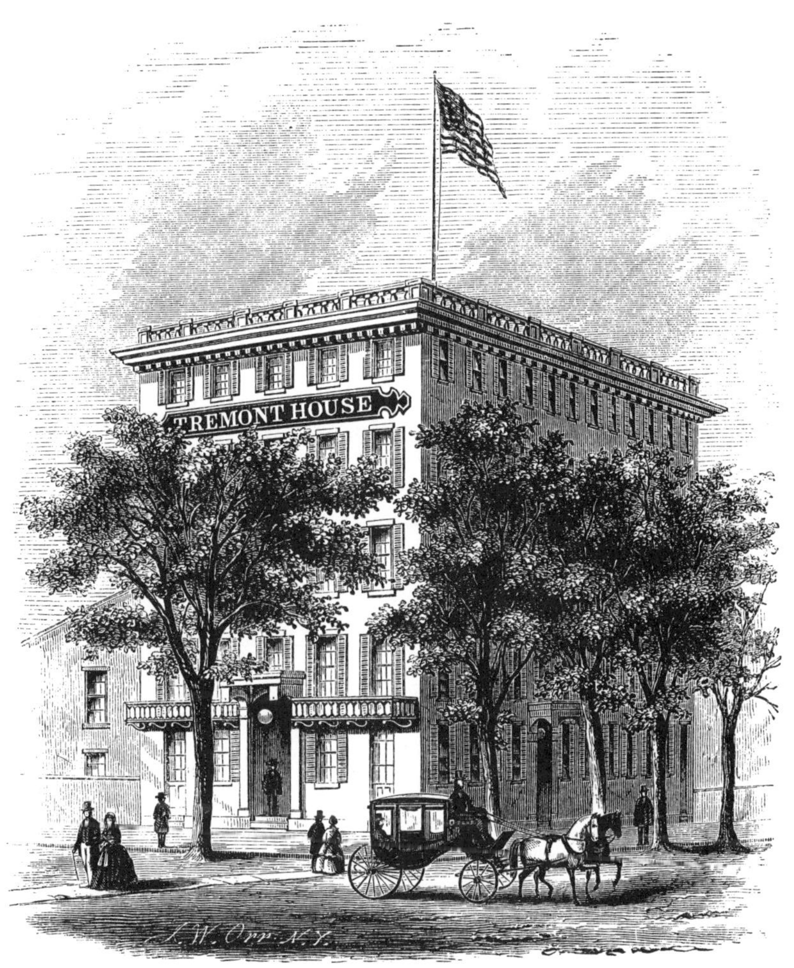

TREMONT HOUSE.

Corner of Court and Orange Streets,

NEW HAVEN, CONN.

ENOS FOOT, Proprietor.

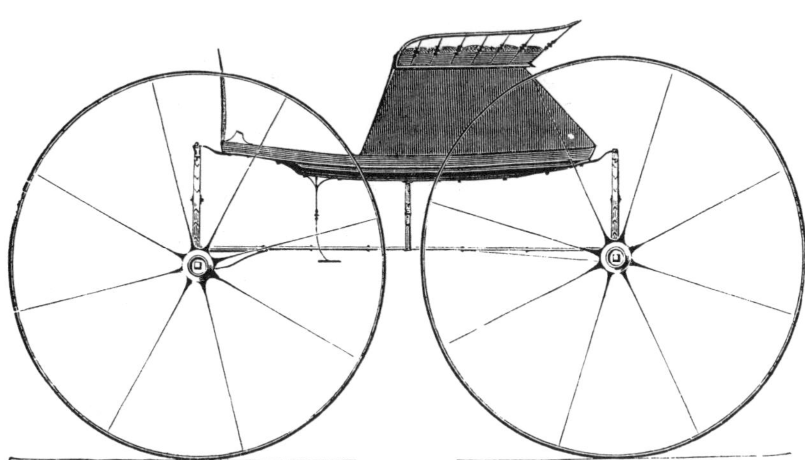

No. 217.—Every Day No-Top Buggie.

No. 218.—English Brougham Rockaway.

No. 219.—American Socaible Rockaway.

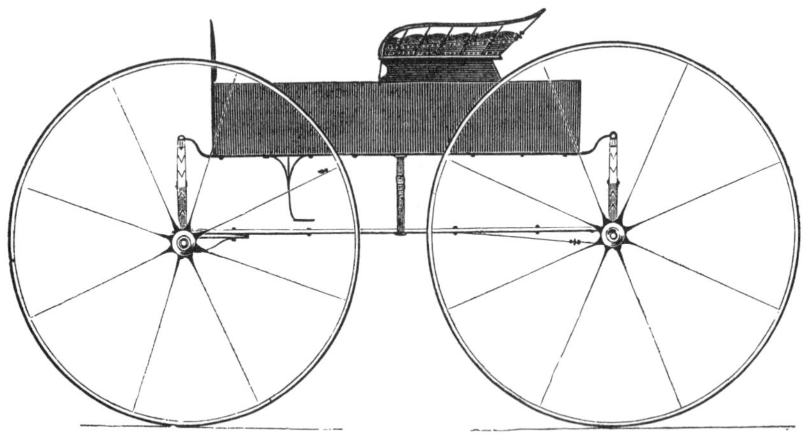

No. 220.—York Wagon.

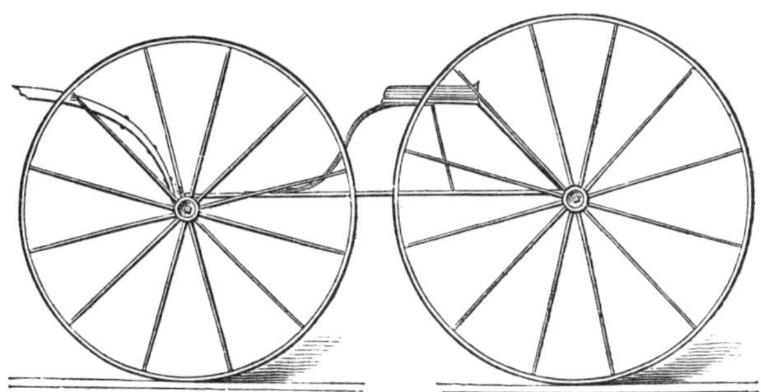

No. 221.—Skeleton Wagon.

No. 222.—Light Curtain Sociable Rockaway.

No. 223.—Brougham Rockaway.

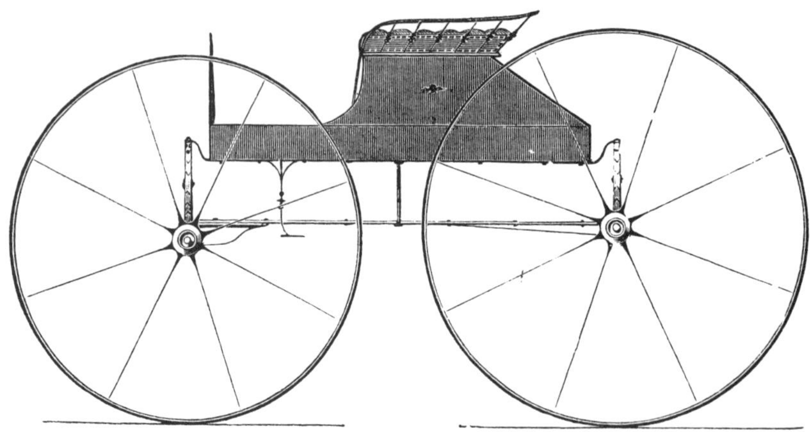

No. 224.—Light Box No-Top Buggie.

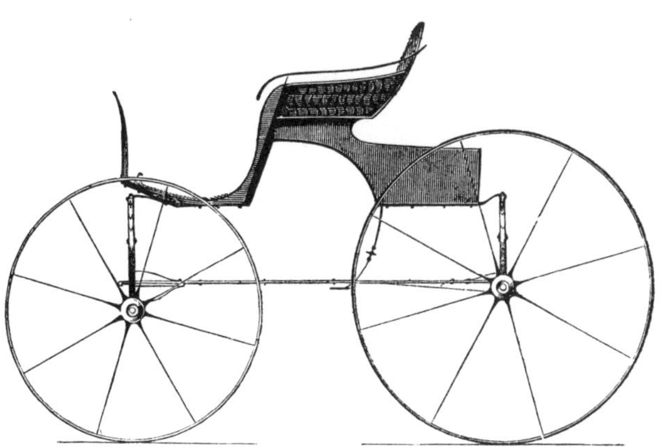

No. 225.—Pony Buggie.

No. 226.—American Socaible Rockaway.

No. 227.—O G Turn Over Seat Rockaway.

No. 228.—Georgia No-Top Buggie.

No. 229.—Legion No-Top Buggie.

No. 230.—Light Columbian Rockaway.

No. 231.—Four-Seat Germantown Rockaway.

No. 232.—Concord No-Top Buggie.

No. 233.—Medium No-Top Buggie.

No. 234.—Scroll Four-Seat Curtain Rockaway.

No. 235.—Compass Four-Seat Curtain Rockaway.

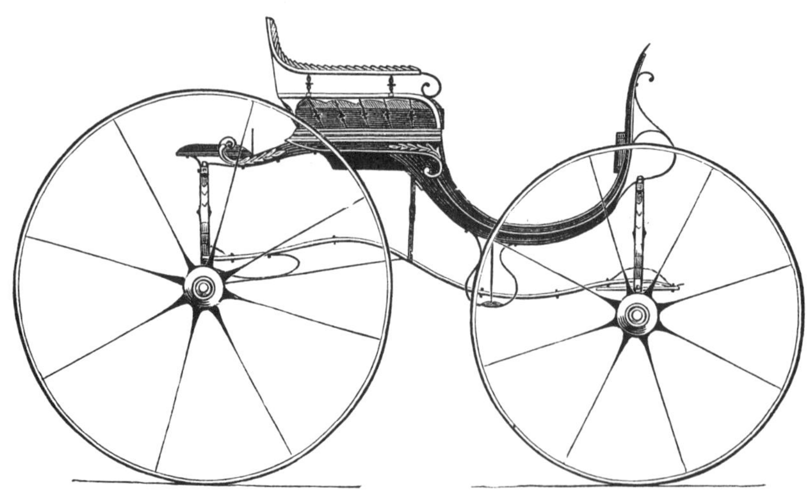

No. 236.—Tilbury No-Top Buggie.

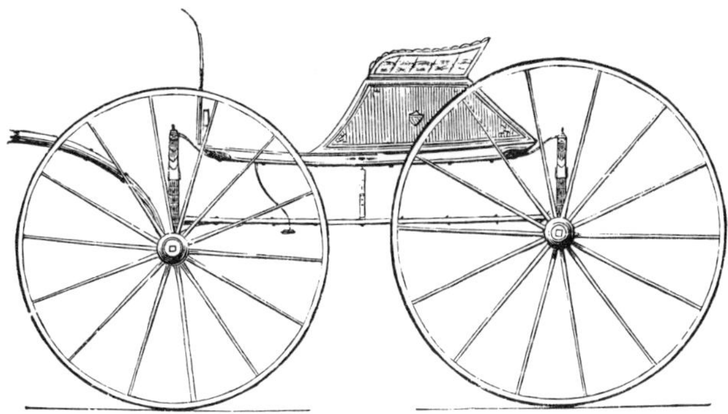

No. 237.—Philadelphia No-Top Buggie.

No. 238.—Light Eureka, Turn-Out Seat, Curtain Rockaway.

No. 239.—Light No-Top Business Wagon.

No. 240.—Movable Top Jagger Wagon.

GEORGE M. PATCHEN, the "Champion Trotting Stallion."

Owned by Dr. Longstreet, of Bordentown, N. J., and Mr. Hall, of Rochester, N. Y.

PATCHEN is a deep blood bay stallion, full 16 hands high. Was foaled in 1849; got by the well-known stallion Cassius M. Clay. Dam, a celebrated Trustee mare—her dam by American Eclipse. He was placed in the stud at Bordentown, in 1852, where he remained, with a brief exception, until 1858. During the latter year he was matched with several fast horses of the New Jersey Course, and defeated most of them with ease. In 1859 Patchen trotted in several matches, on Long Island, with marked success, defeating many well-known horses—among which were the following: Pilot, Brown Dick, Miller's Damsel, Lady Woodruff, and Lancet. In May, 1860, Patchen clearly demonstrated his superior trotting powers by defeating, in two races, the famous Ethan Allen; but the zenith of his glory was not reached until his memorable contest with Flora Temple, on the 12th of June, 1860, in which he defeated that world-renowned trotter, making his mile in 2:23—the fastest trotting time ever made by a stallion on the American Turf.

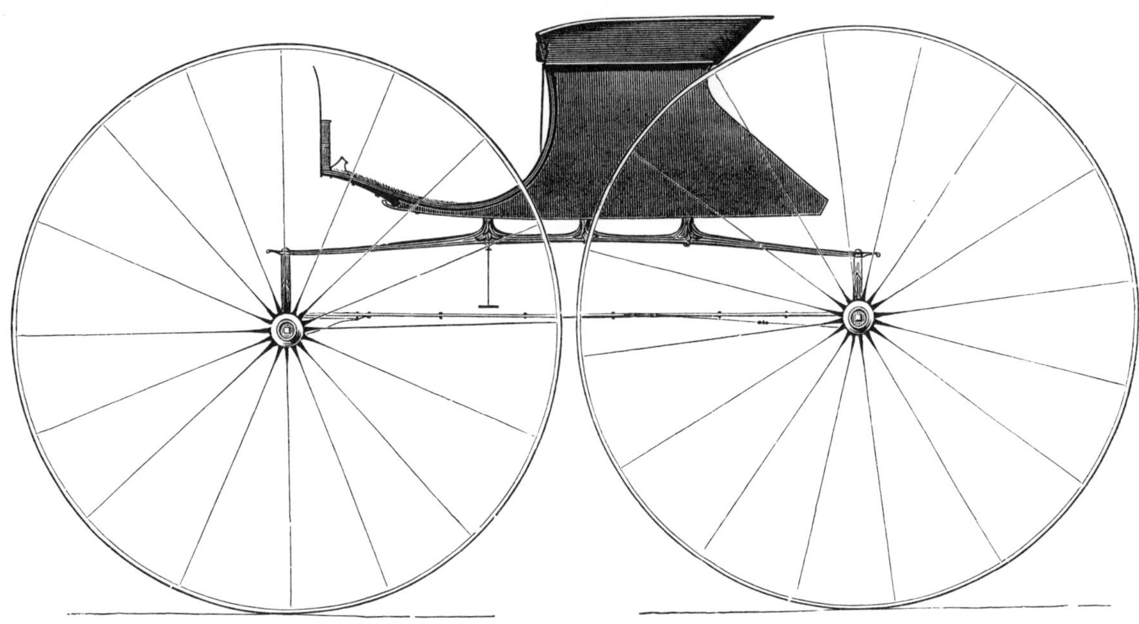

No. 241.—Beauty, No-Top Trotter.

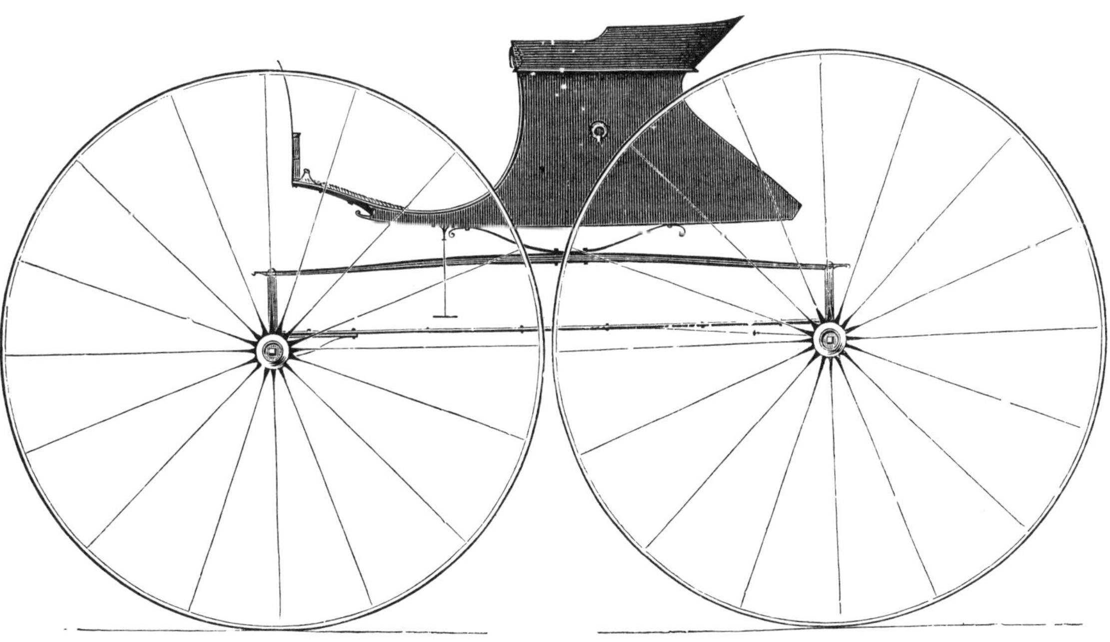

No. 242.—Handsome No-Top Trotter.

No. 243.
Quinnipiack Jump Seat Rockaway.

No. 244.—Continental Top Buggie.

No. 245.—Shifting Top Tilbury.

No. 246.—Quinnipiack Jump Seat Rockaway.

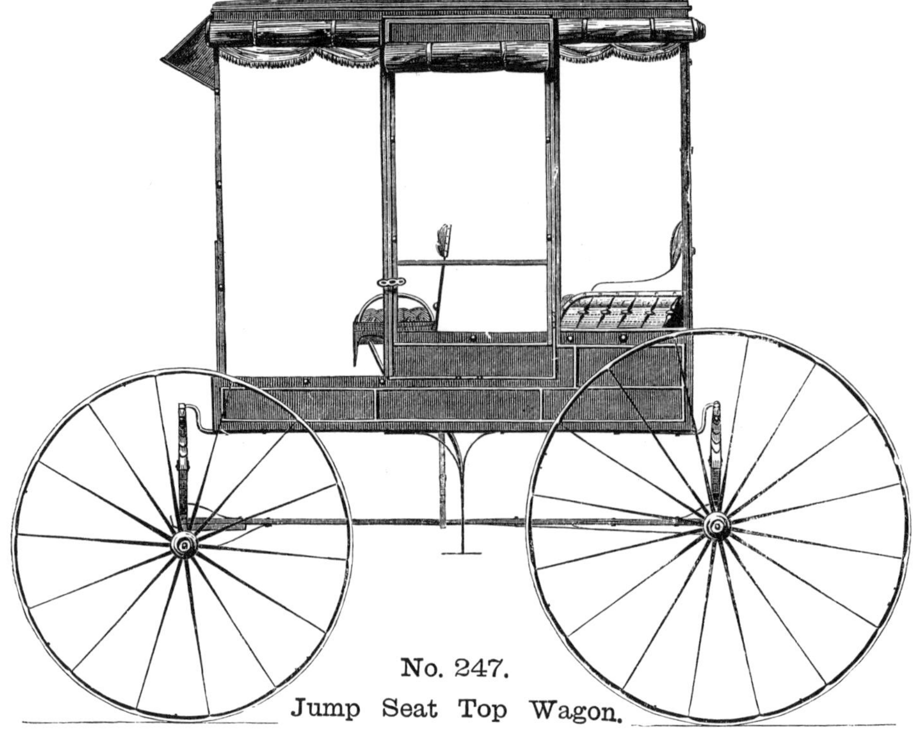

No. 247.
Jump Seat Top Wagon.

No. 248.—Prince Albert Buggie.

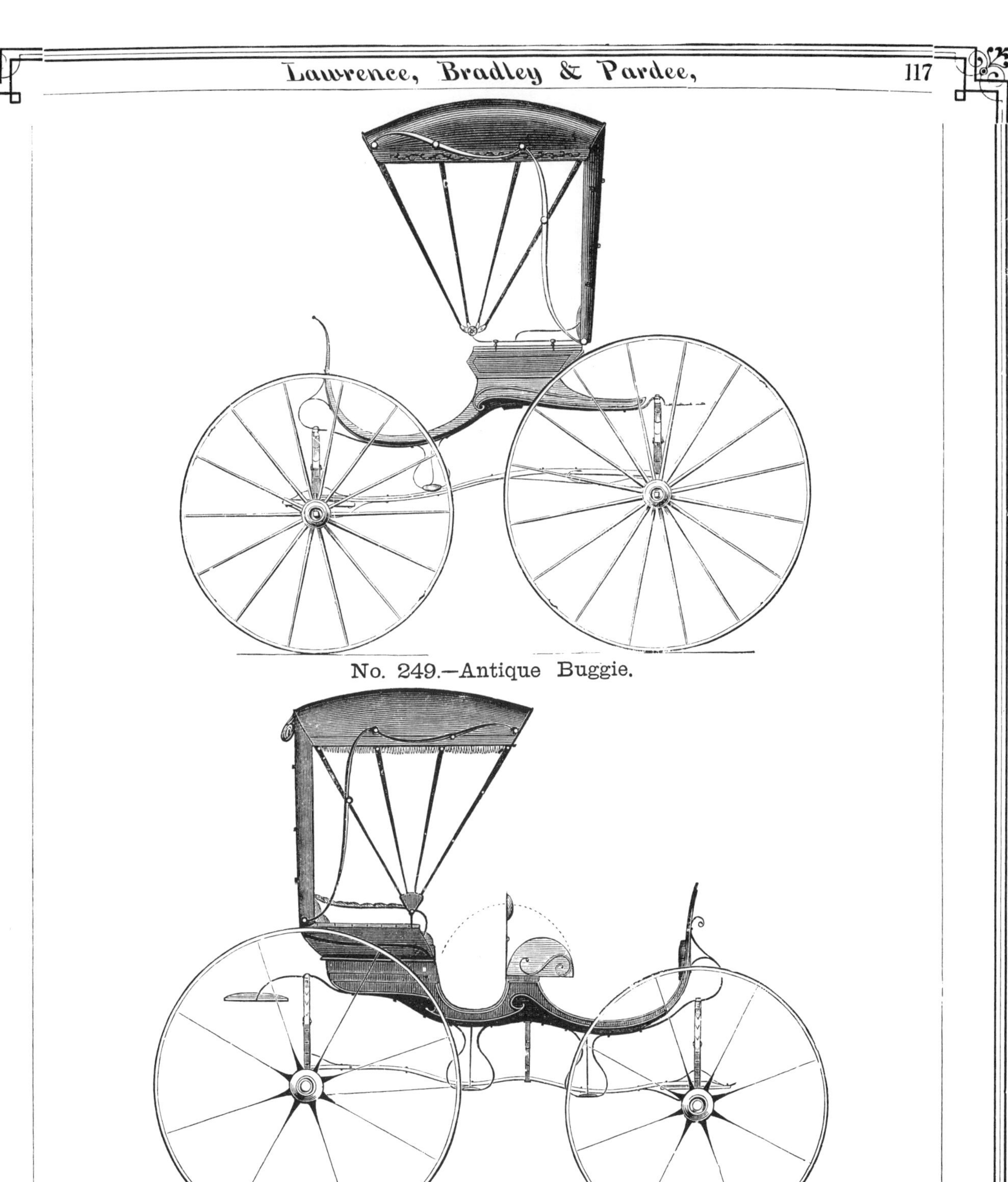

No. 249.—Antique Buggie.

No. 250.—Slide Seat Buggie.

No. 251.—Closed Extension Top Side Seat Buggie.

No. 252.—Cash Buggie.

No. 253.—Concord Top Buggie.

No. 254.—Open Extension-Top Slide Seat.

No. 255.—Box Slide-Seat Buggie.

No. 256.—Tilbury Buggie.

No. 257.—Universal Box-Buggie.

No 258—Turn-Out Seat Box-Buggie.

No. 259.—Shifting-Top Turn-Out-Seat Buggie.

No. 260.—Park Phaeton.

No. 261.—Cut-Under Buggie

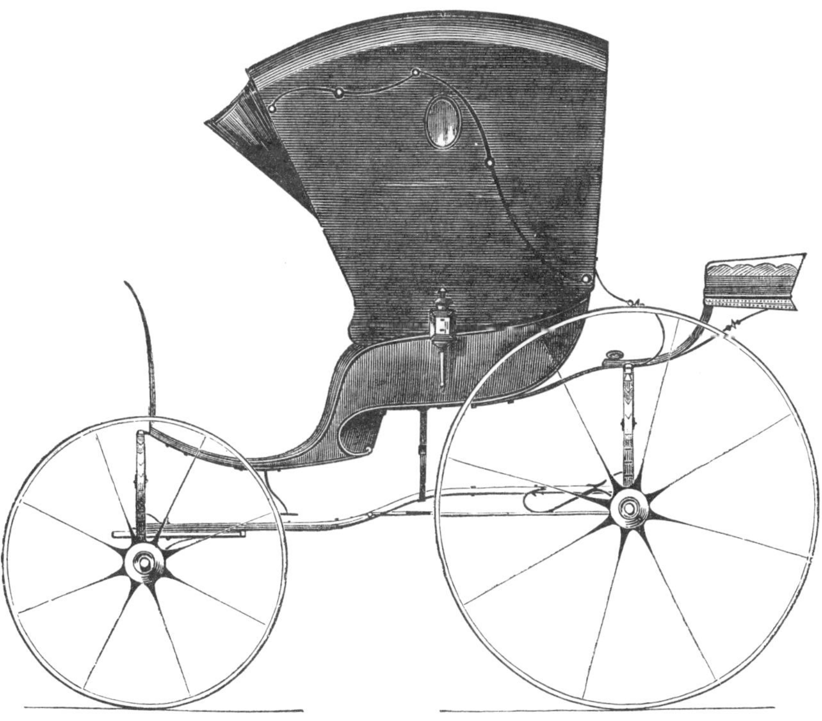

No. 262.—Doctor's Heavy Phaeton.

No. 263.—Drop-Front Turn-Out-Seat Buggie.

No. 264.—Turn-Out-Seat Buggie.

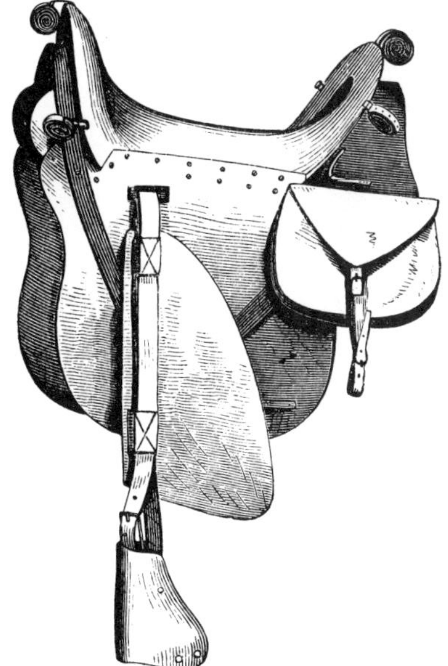

No. 9.— McClellan.

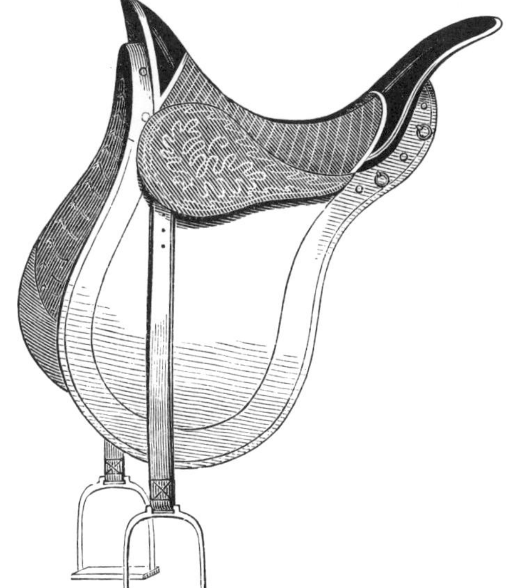

No. 10.—Dragoon.

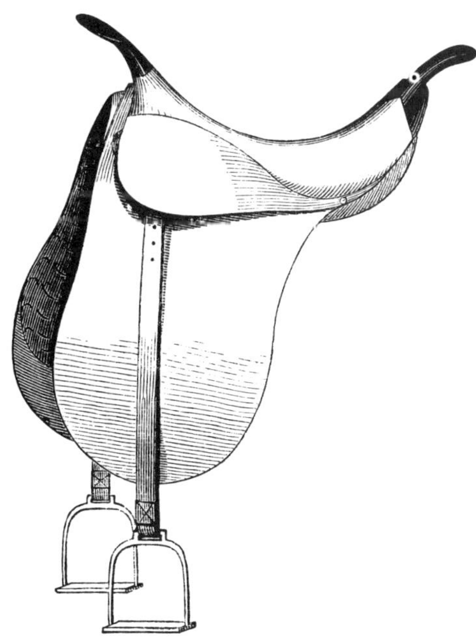

No. 11.—Half Hussar.

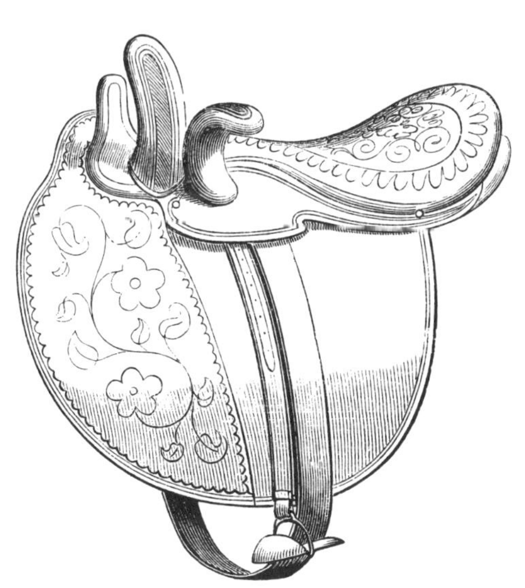

No. 12.— Leaping Horn Side.

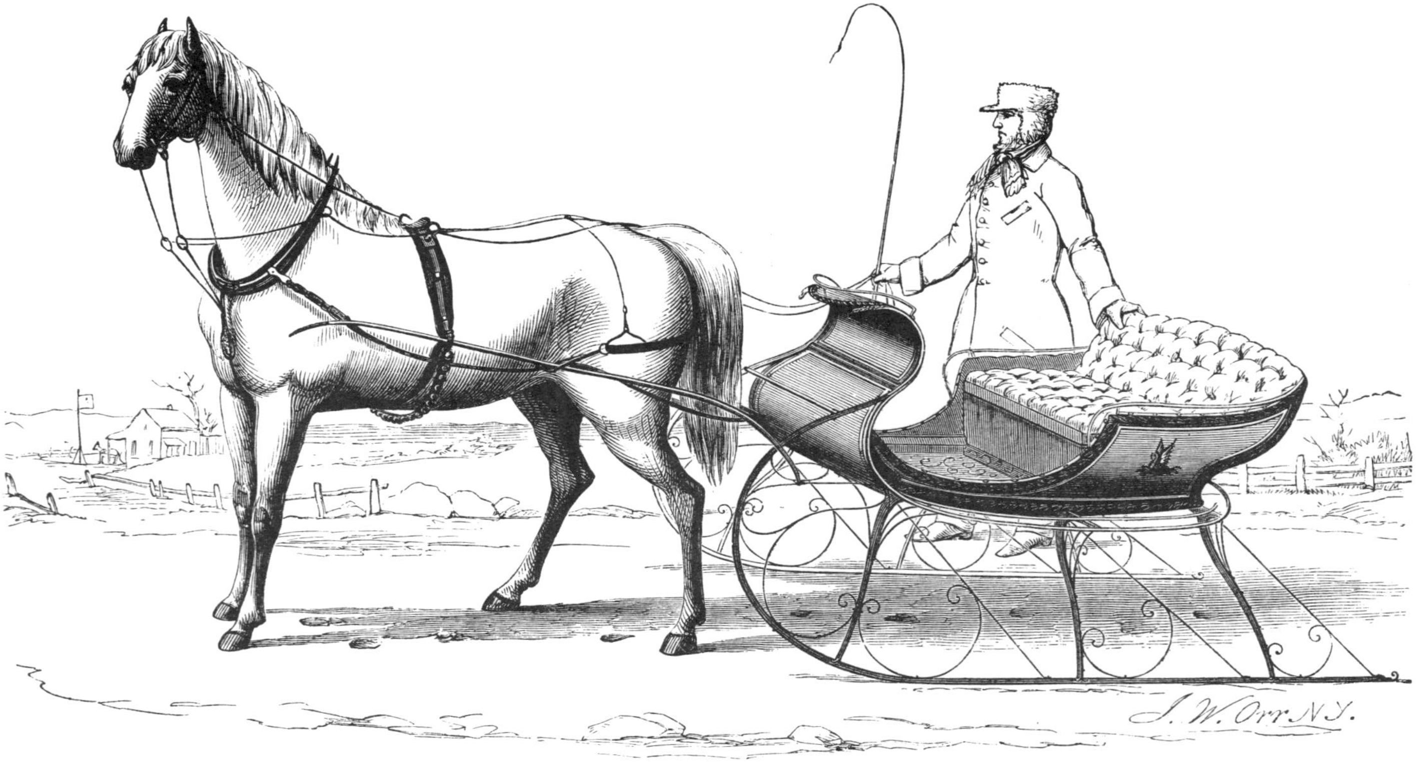

S. W. Orr N.Y.

No. 265.—Portland Sleigh.

No. 266.--C Spring Brainard Gig.

No. 267.—Spanish Prince Albert.

No. 268.—Eureka Jump-Seat

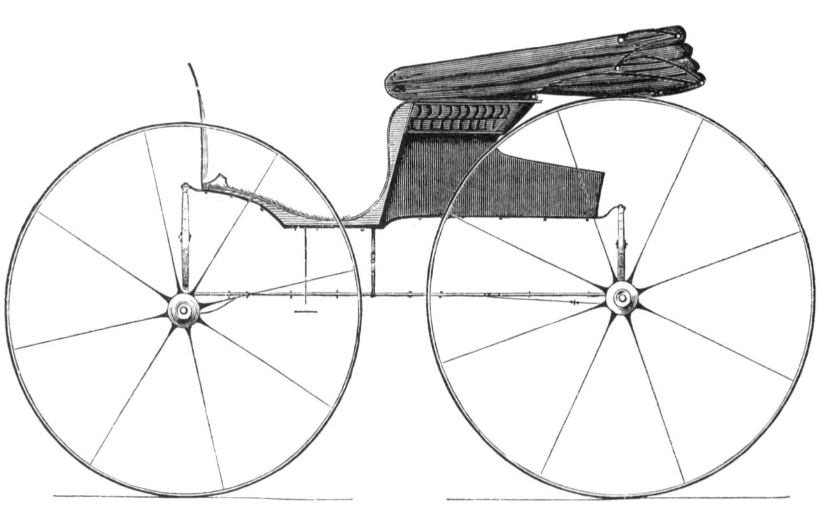

No. 269.—Common-Sense Buggie.

No. 270 —Doctor's York-Phaeton.

271.—Eureka Jump-Seat Buggie.

No. 272.—New Orleans Jump-Seat Buggie.

273.—Standing-Top Doctor's-Phaeton.

No. 274.—Gazelle Cut-Under Buggie.

No. 275.—New Orleans Jump-Seat Buggie.

No. 276.—Extension-Top Jump-Seat Buggie.

No. 277.—Light Shifting-Top Box-Buggie.

No. 278.—Queen's Phaeton.

No. 279.—Extension-Top Jump-Seat Buggie.

No. 280.—Box Jump-Seat Buggie.

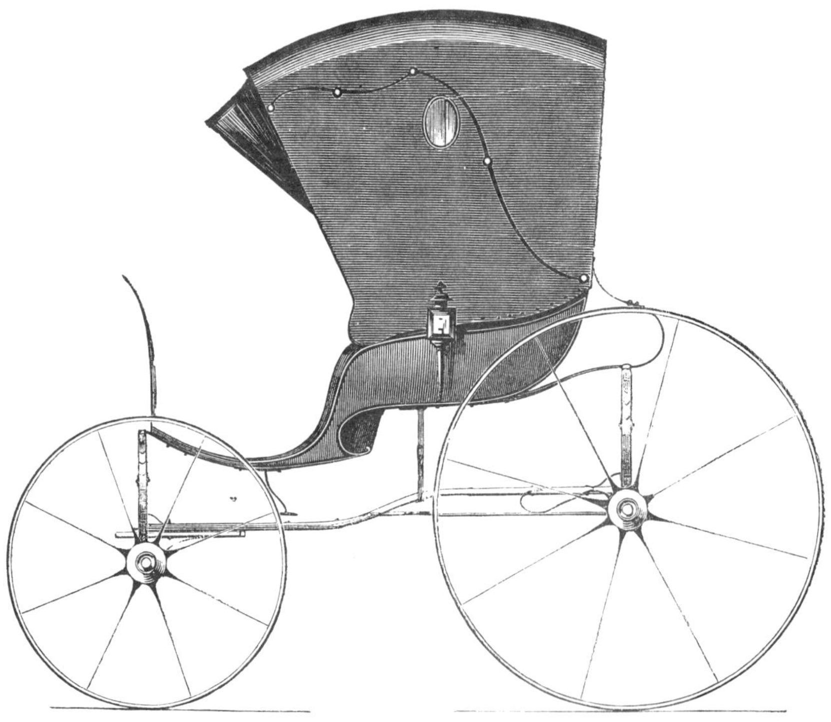

No. 281.—Full-Size Phaeton.

No. 282.—English Prince Albert.

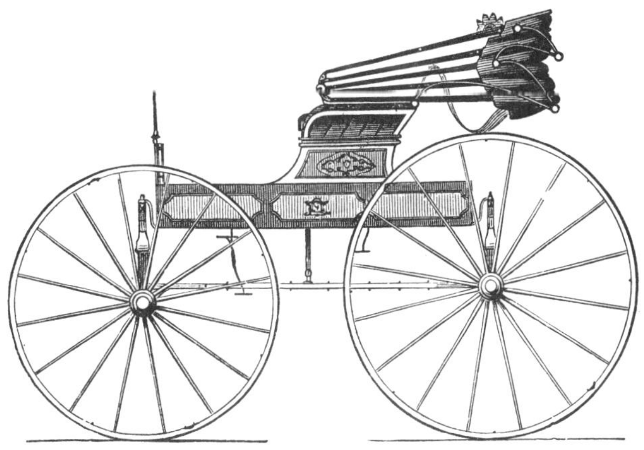

No. 283.—Box Jump-Seat Buggie.

No. 284.—Draw-Front Phaeton.

285.—Sensible Buggie.

No. 286.—Deep-Side Box-Buggie.

No. 287.—Draw-Front Phaeton.

No. 288.—Superior Top-Buggie.

No. 289.—Light Brainard Gig.

NEW HAVEN HOUSE
J. W. Orr. N.Y.

No. 290.--Every-Day Buggie.

291.—Excelsior Trotter.

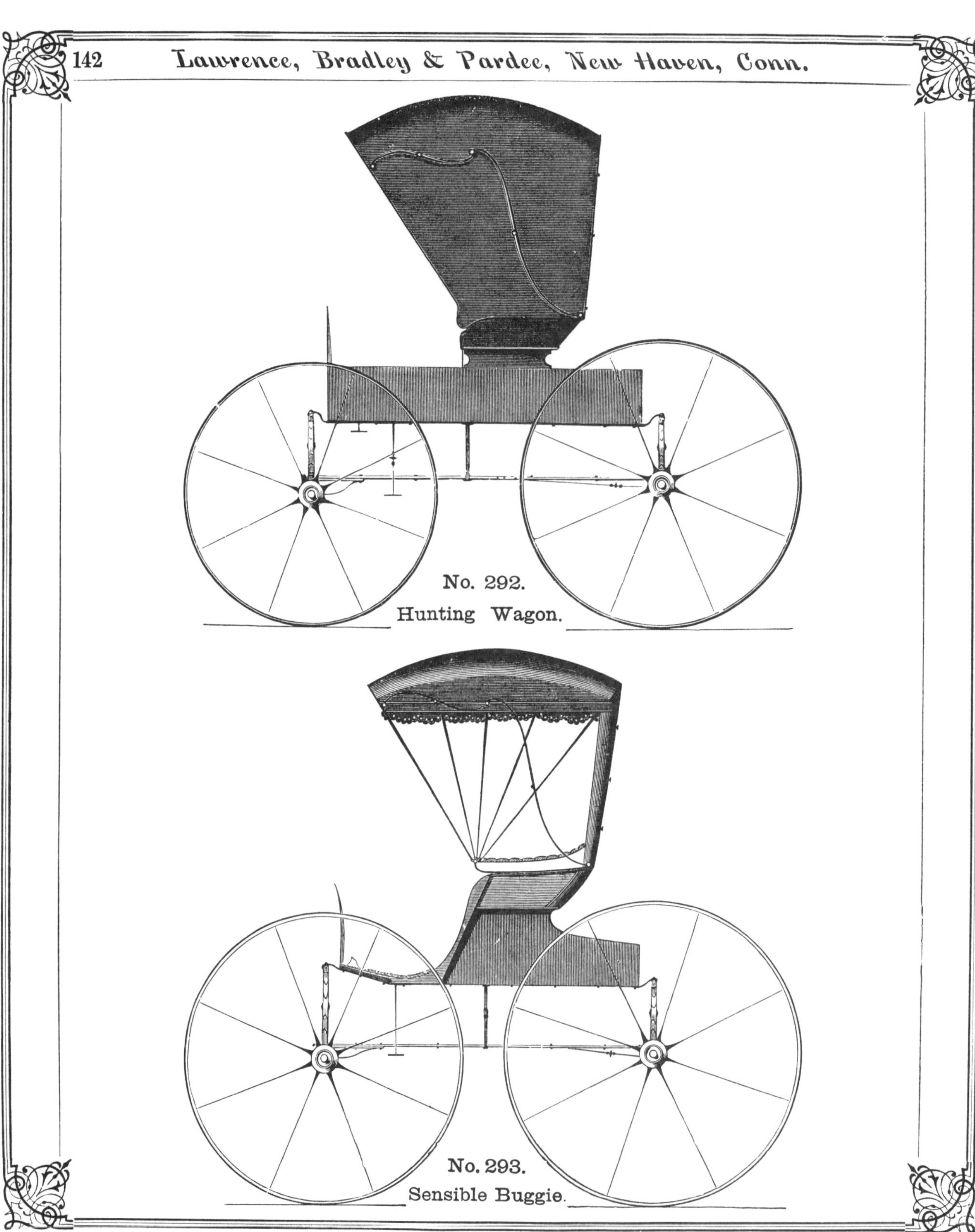

No. 292.
Hunting Wagon.

No. 293.
Sensible Buggie.

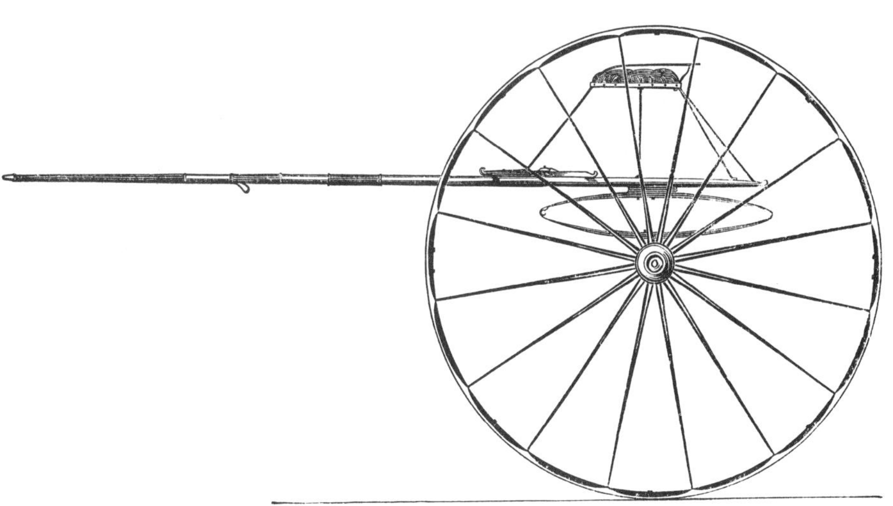

No. 294.—Road Sulky

No. 295.—Boston Chaise.

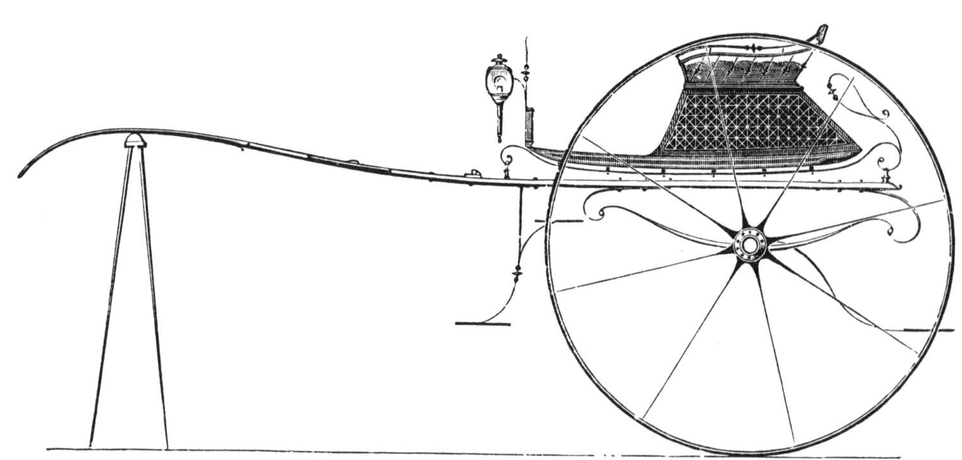

No. 296.—Stanhope.

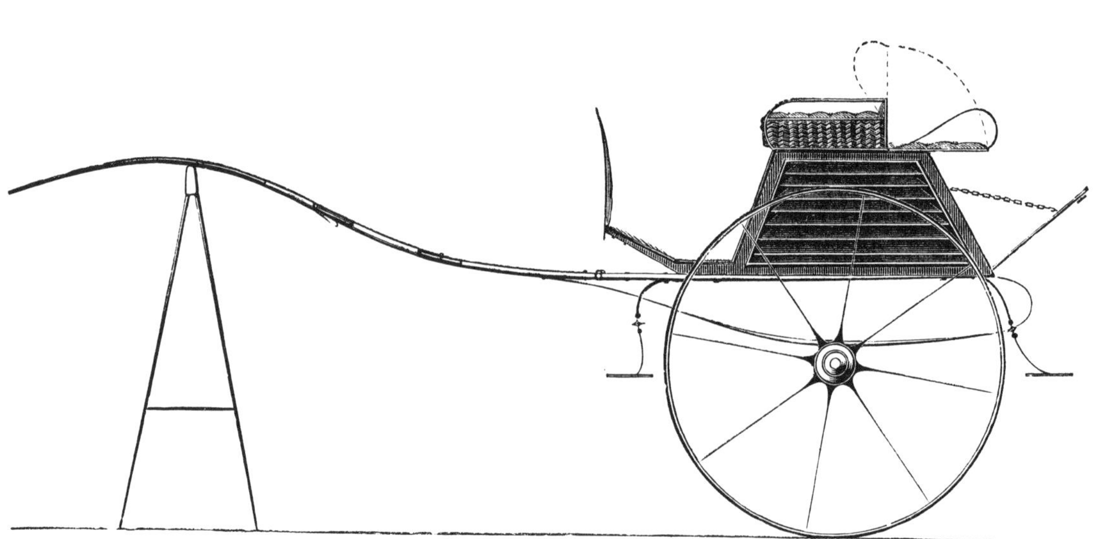

No. 297.—Light French Dog-Cart.

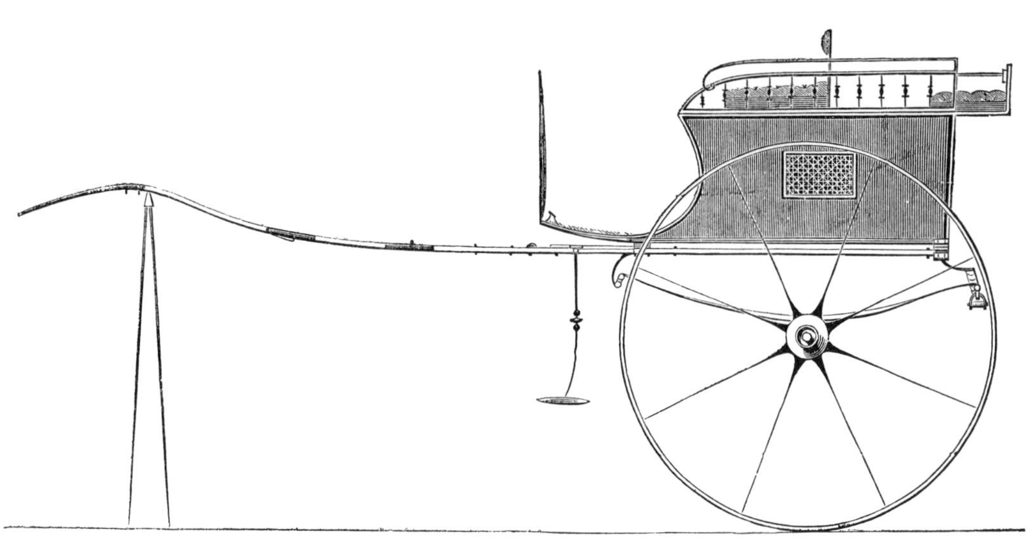

No. 298.—Barnsbury Cart.

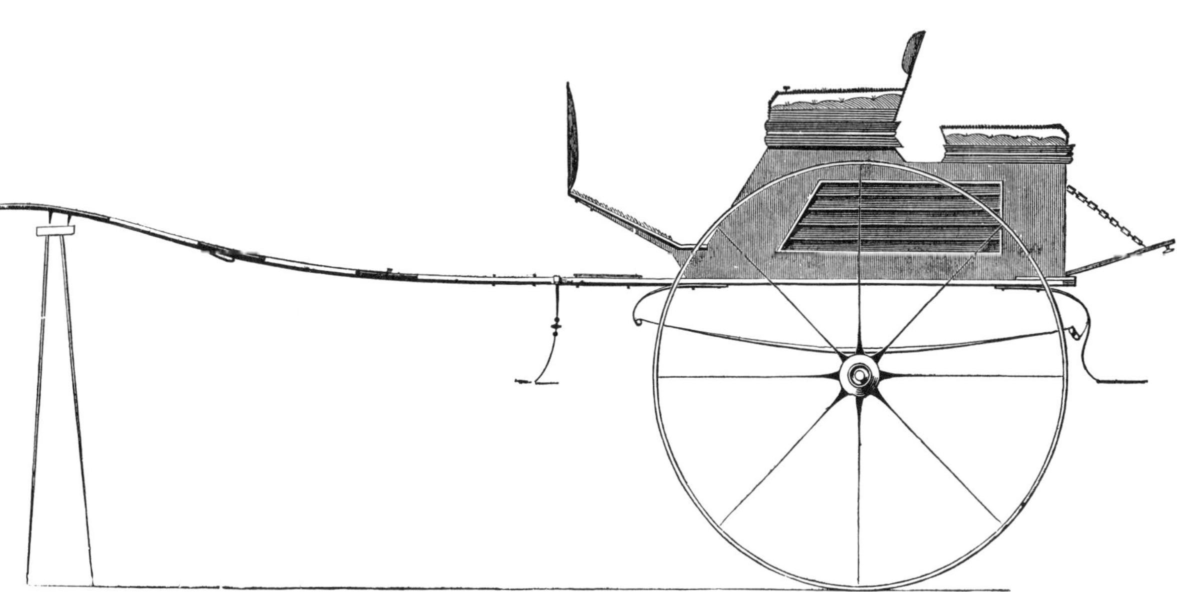

No. 299.—English Dog-Cart.

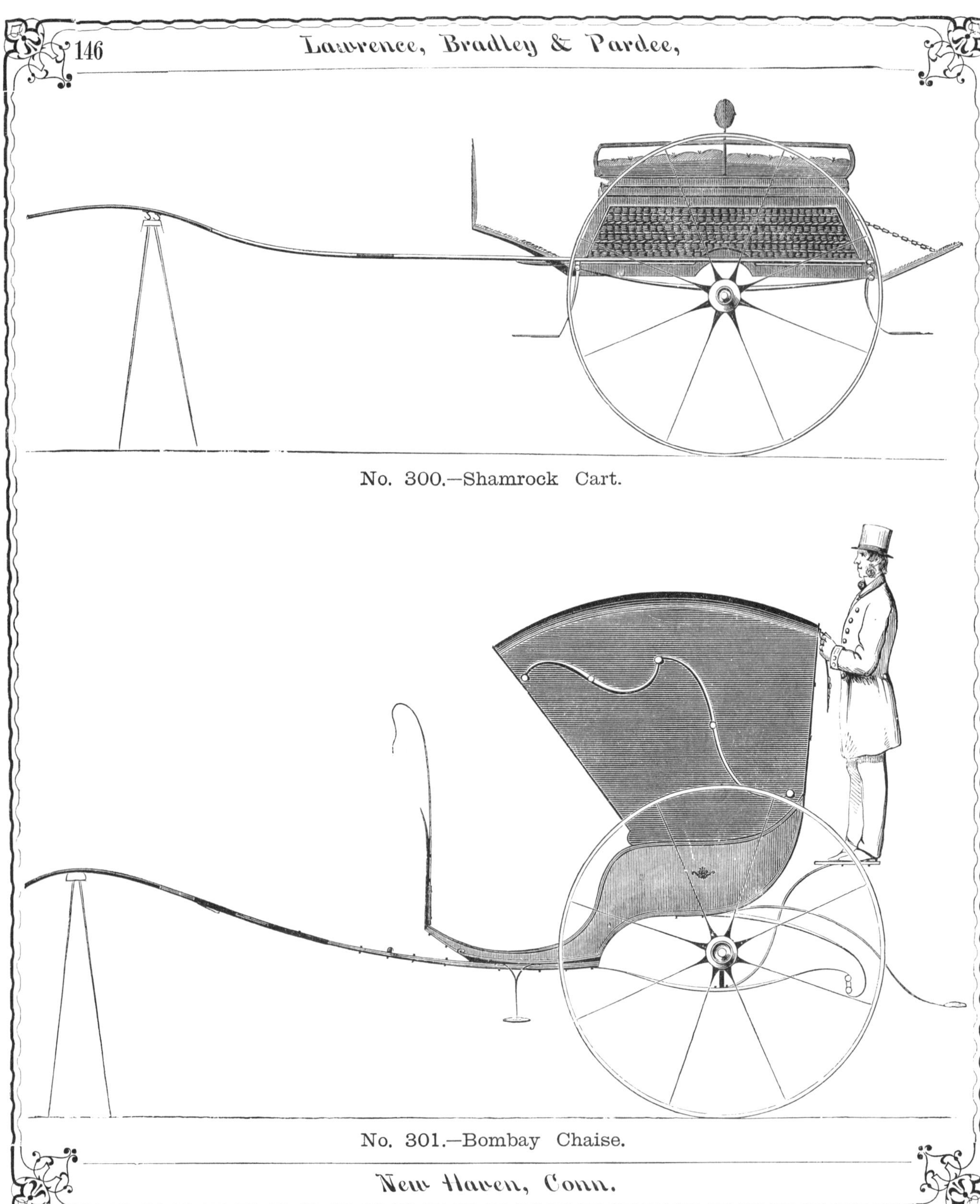

No. 300.—Shamrock Cart.

No. 301.—Bombay Chaise.

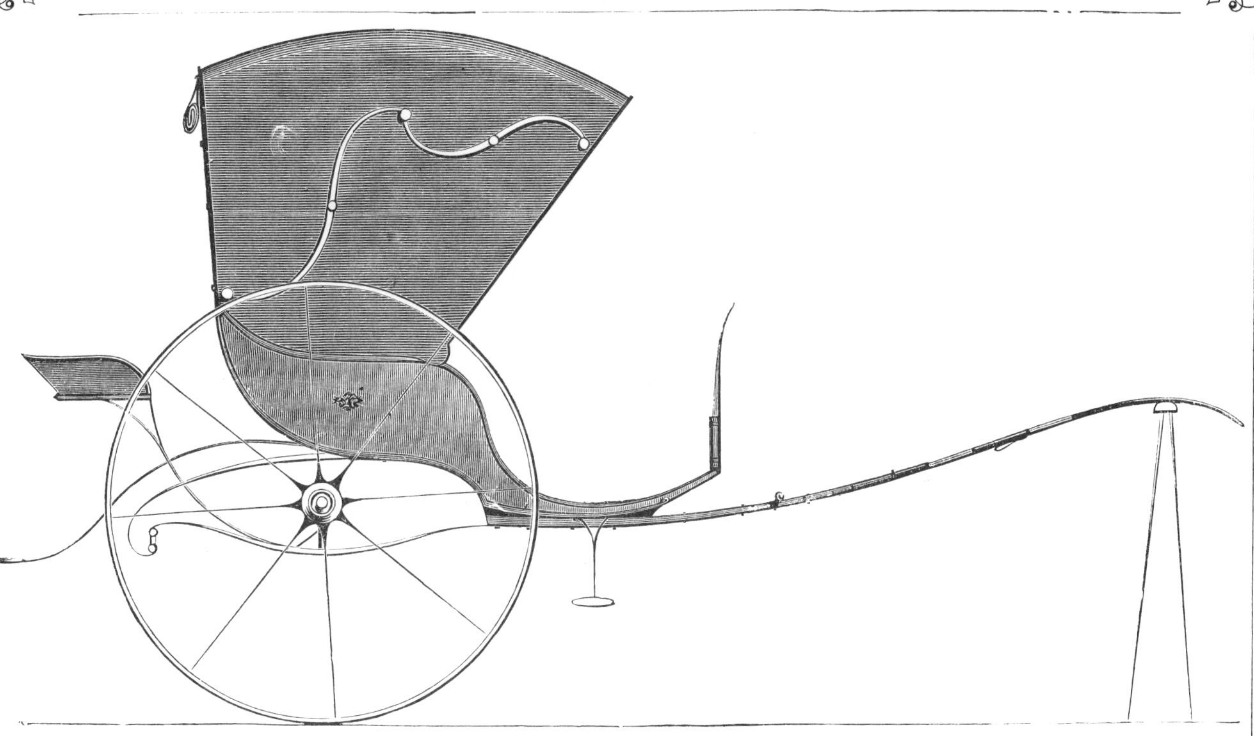

No. 302.—Bombay Chaise.

No. 303.—Step Chaise.

NEW HAVEN STEAMBOAT LINE,

FARE—ONE DOLLAR. NO CHARGE FOR BERTHS.

The First-Class Steamer

CONTINENTAL,

CAPT. J. M. LEWIS,

Will leave New York every day (Sundays excepted), at 3 o'clock P. M. Returning, leave New Haven daily, at 11 o'clock P. M.

CONTINENTAL

CONTINENTAL

J. W. Orr, N. Y.

NIGHT LINE.

The Steamer "**ELM CITY**," Capt. J. G. BOWNS, will leave New York every night at 11 o'clock (Sundays excepted). Returning, leaves New Haven every morning at $10\frac{1}{4}$ o'clock. TIME, $4\frac{1}{2}$ hours.

RICHARD PECK, Agent.

Office No. 31 *Peck Slip, corner of Front Street.*